Where Two or Three Are Gathered

Where Two or Three
ARE GATHERED

Spiritual Direction for Small Groups

Daniel L. Prechtel

Morehouse Publishing
NEW YORK · HARRISBURG · DENVER

Morehouse Publishing, 4775 Linglestown Road, Harrisburg, PA 17112

Morehouse Publishing, 445 Fifth Avenue, New York, NY 10016

Morehouse Publishing is an imprint of Church Publishing Incorporated.
www.churchpublishing.org

Cover design by Laurie Klein Westhafer
Typeset by Vicki K. Black

Library of Congress Cataloging-in-Publication Data

Prechtel, Daniel L.
Where two or three are gathered : spiritual direction for small groups /
Daniel L. Prechtel.
     p.   cm.
Includes bibliographical references and index.
ISBN 978-0-8192-2772-0 (pbk.: alk. paper) — ISBN 978-0-8192-2773-7
(ebook) 1. Spiritual direction—Christianity. 2. Small groups. 3. Church group
work. I. Title.
BV5053.P74 2012
253.5'3—dc23   2012001456

Printed in the United States of America

10   9   8   7   6   5   4   3   2   1

Contents

Acknowledgments

I AM DEEPLY GRATEFUL to the many communities that have supported me in my spiritual life and given me the opportunity to lead and learn, to make mistakes and grow from them, to discover grace and celebrate how the ordinary shimmers with the holy. I am particularly grateful to Seabury-Western Theological Seminary where I had the wonderful experience of teaching and coaching small groups with students for nine years, the Institute of Spiritual Companionship and its pilot class in Group Spiritual Companionship, and the many people I have companioned as individuals, in groups, or in training programs through Lamb & Lion Spiritual Guidance Ministries.

Students in my courses in spiritual guidance with the Center of Anglican Learning and Leadership (CALL) program at Church Divinity School of the Pacific and in the small-group leaders training program at All Souls Episcopal Parish in Berkeley helped me further develop this work. Thanks also to colleagues who took the time to look over drafts of this book.

Finally, I offer a special note of gratitude to Ruth Meyers, who has generously given me love and support, including lending me her editorial eyes. I am so fortunate to have her as my spouse, dear friend, and spiritual companion.

Introduction

SPIRITUAL COMPANIONSHIP small groups have played a major role in my life. After I wandered in my own inner wilderness for much of my late teens and twenties, a small group of older members of the church I had recently joined took me into their midst and loved me into spiritual sanity. The Tuesday Night Liturgy Group was a quirky affair consisting of what they considered an avant-garde worship experience followed by a shared meal. But the ritual of offbeat worship, meal, and conversation served to bring me in from my isolation and give me a sense of belonging to an intimate community. Here I could be known and know others, and I felt free to share the ups and downs of my life as a young man with a child and wife and a social services job. Here, I experienced a major spiritual turning point and attempted to live intentionally as a Christian. The group was a godsend.

The late 1960s was a time of social, political, and spiritual turbulence in the United States. As the façade of Christendom began to crack, Eastern gurus promised direct encounters with the Divine. I had been a member of a Protestant church that primarily set rules of moral conduct and suggested a view of God that seemed distant and transcendent. I learned things *about* God, but did not find much guidance on how to *be with* God in this life. I can't blame that pastor or the church—many places were like that, and unfortunately still are. But I yearned for encounter with the Divine and began practicing Eastern-style meditation at the age of seventeen. Then one time when I was nineteen years old the music of a river near an open field where I was walking and the diamond-like clarity of a starry night caught me by surprise. I felt an invitation to join in the dance of the cosmos. I was caught up in that dance for twenty minutes or so and was then left wondering whether

1

I had experienced some form of mystical unity or had simply gone wonderfully, ecstatically, nuts.

It shook me up. I went to my parents and then to my pastor but no one could help me make sense of what I had experienced. The Protestant tradition I was embedded in did not (at that time at least) have a way to guide me and connect me to Christians on a spiritual journey that included that type of unitive experience. So I left the religion of my parents and embarked on a perilous spiritual journey without a guide. In the process of my exploration I learned many things about the reality of the spiritual dimension of life, but it was costly to me and to those around me.

When I bottomed out from self-centered spirituality, the acquisition of personal power, and drug abuse and was open to revisiting Christian beliefs and practices, many of my family had joined an Episcopal church. In testing out that setting for myself I discovered several things. One discovery was that the symbols and sacraments that are part of the liturgy and the life of the church spoke powerfully to me in a way that discursive, rational thought and study alone could not.

I also learned that there is a whole treasury of mystical and spiritual writings in Christianity, developed over many centuries, that I hadn't known existed. In some branches of Protestantism there was the temptation to throw out anything that was pre-Reformation or had connection with Catholic or Orthodox tradition. However, in Episcopal/Anglican tradition the historical links and dialogues with other Christian traditions remained.

There were, I discovered, small-group and spiritual direction resources available to me for guidance and spiritual support.[1] As I explored the opportunities for group spiritual companionship and spiritual direction, I wanted to offer these to others as well as receive them myself. Because of my own experience, I did not want other seekers and spiritual explorers to have to make their spiritual journey alone and without guidance.

I started leading spiritual companionship groups as a lay member of my church, and then in my first year at seminary I began receiving spiritual direction while also being a member of several small support groups. As a parish priest in a small church in Michigan, I encouraged the development of small groups as well as led some for particular seasons of the church year. I brought back from The Upper Room's Academy for Spiritual Formation a model for covenant groups and helped some of the men in the parish start such a group. I also developed my *Circle of the Spirit* group model as an Academy project, and then presented a *Dreamwork* group approach for some parishioners and others outside the church.[2] By that time I was also leading retreats and providing spiritual direction on a part-time basis.

In 1995 my wife, Ruth Meyers, accepted a teaching position in Evanston, Illinois, at Seabury-Western Theological Seminary, and I moved from parish ministry and founded Lamb & Lion Spiritual Guidance Ministries to focus on spiritual direction and related ministries.[3] I was invited in 1996 to join the staff and faculty of the Institute of Spiritual Companionship and served that institute in various capacities. Seabury-Western invited me to teach the Spiritual Formation in Small Groups series from 2000 until 2009. That was a time of fruitful experimentation in developing models of spiritual companionship with my students. In 2004 I led a nine-month training program in Group Spiritual Leadership through Lamb & Lion Spiritual Guidance Ministries, and adapted that as program director for the Group Spiritual Companionship academic year program for the Institute of Spiritual Companionship in 2008–09. The former members of these formation programs and classes now include ordained ministers and lay leaders working in churches, chaplains in hospitals, a professional writer on spiritual themes, a guide and spiritual director for wilderness retreats, a psychotherapist in private practice, spiritual directors, and professionals in health-care institutions. Since that time at Seabury and the Institute of Spiritual Companionship, my wife and I moved to the San Francisco Bay area and I am exploring new opportunities for teaching about and leading spiritual companionship groups, including through the Internet.

This book is my offering to all who desire useful models for group spiritual companionship and a resource for developing leaders of these groups. Spiritual companionship small groups provide important spiritual and emotional holding environments for community belonging, give members windows into their souls, and invite their attention to the Presence (or the Spirit, or other language for the Divine) in their midst. Those who will find these small-group models useful include spiritual directors and spiritual companions, parish priests and church ministers, lay ministers inside and outside the church, counselors and therapists, and chaplains, among others. This book does not stand alone, even though it is intended to be a primary text for forming spiritual companionship group leaders. So I have included extensive references to other resources that will complement the book and expand upon its presentation.

Although I use the phrase *spiritual companionship group,* all of these groups also have a spiritual direction component. There is a fundamental emphasis on attending to the Presence within the group, bringing new insight, direction, and wisdom leading toward a greater wholeness for its members. Since the leader facilitates attentiveness to the Presence and discernment of God's movements within the group and its members, she or he is practicing spiritual direction with the group. Consequently, we also can call the kinds of small groups described herein various forms of spiritual direction groups.

Chapter 1 provides sociological findings on small groups, and then lays historical, theological, and psychospiritual groundwork for understanding group spiritual dynamics. In chapter 2 I discuss the elements that are at the common core of these small groups, even though there are many variations that the group may take. I have provided a wide variety of models of small groups along with pertinent background information, and have clustered the group models into several categories. Small groups where members explore sharing a spiritual practice or exercise that is introduced by the leader are the focus of chapter 3. These group formats include *Circle of the Spirit, Holy Reading,* and *Contemplative Prayer.*

In chapter 4 I introduce groups that emphasize cultivating inner awareness and discernment, including *Spiritual Friends, Dreamwork,* and *Communal Dreaming.* Groups that focus on building a spiritual community of support, such as *Benedictine Community* and *Companions in Transition,* are discussed in chapter 5. In chapter 6 we look at groups that emphasize compassion and social action, especially *Healing Prayer* and *Covenant for Justice and Peace* group models.

A deeper discussion of leadership qualities and considerations for facilitating these small groups is found in chapter 7. The reader will find a model of a leaders' peer supervision and consultation group, as well as information on starting a parish-based small-group program. Also, we will look at special applications of group spiritual direction leadership to other settings—retreats, organizational spiritual guidance, interfaith and secular group settings, and long-distance and virtual Internet groups. At the end of each model in chapters 3–6 and at the end of chapter 7, I offer suggestions of helpful resources.

Following the conclusion of the book is an appendix that offers spiritual exercises and practices that I have found helpful for leading *Circle of the Spirit* groups or retreats. Some of those exercises are of my own creation, while others come from other sources.

It is my hope that people of religious traditions other than Christianity will find this book to be a useful resource as well. I am deeply appreciative of the whole community of faiths. My ecumenical and interfaith partners in spiritual companionship have been truly and deeply enriching to me. It is my sincere hope that, while the language and experience is primarily from the perspective of an ordained Christian priest who loves his tradition and is firmly rooted in it, the spirit of an interfaith approach to developing spiritual companionship groups shines through the text. Therefore, I offer this book in the spirit of the Spirit that is shared by all the tents pitched on the common ground of the community of faiths and never fully contained by any of them.

chapter one

The Power of Small Groups for Spiritual Companionship

The Importance of Small Groups

Small groups provide a powerful support for and influence on people. We are not made, as the Genesis creation story says, to be alone. We are hard-wired for community. Consider the popular television shows that mirrored our desire for support, belonging, and a safe place to reflect on our lives and interact with intimacy. *Cheers,* a show that ran from 1982 to 1993, is set in the local tavern, the place "where everybody knows your name." *Friends* (1994–2004) picked up a new generation of television viewers with a similar theme and song assuring viewers, "I'll be there for you." These shows were enormously popular because they tapped into our primary need for human community.

In November 1991 the Gallup Organization conducted a national survey of 1,021 people who were members of small groups and 962 who were not members. The findings, summarized in Robert Wuthnow's book *"I Come Away Stronger": How Small Groups Are Shaping American Religion,* speak to how important small groups are for many people in the United States:

- Over half of American adults are now (40 percent) or have been (15 percent) involved in a small group.

- Nearly one-fourth of those not currently involved in a small group would like to join one.

- Nearly six of ten small-group members are part of a church- or synagogue-sponsored group.

- About six of ten say they joined a group because someone they knew invited them.

- A high level of importance and satisfaction is expressed for small groups among the vast majority of members.

- The vast majority of members see small groups as a source of community and personal support.

Those who were members of church-based small groups reported:

- Ninety-seven percent of people in church-based groups say they need to be "part of a group that helps you grow spiritually." Sixty-four percent say this need has been fully met.

- Eighty-four percent say that their faith or spirituality has been influenced from involvement in the group.

- Eighty-six percent say they have "sensed God's presence in the group."

- Ninety percent feel closer to God (33 percent in non-church group [n-c]).

- Eighty-seven percent have a deeper love toward other people (55 percent n-c).

- Eighty-five percent have a better ability to forgive others (53 percent n-c).

- Eighty-two percent have a better ability to forgive themselves (52 percent n-c).

- Eighty-five percent say the Bible has become more meaningful (21 percent n-c).

- Seventy-five percent experienced answers to prayers (25 percent n-c).

- Seventy-five percent feel it helped in "sharing your faith with others outside the group."

Group members also reported other significant benefits:

- Fifty-three percent experienced "healings of relationships."

- Eighty percent worked with the group to help someone inside the group who was in need (65 percent n-c).

- Seventy-two percent worked with the group to help other people in need outside the group (57 percent n-c).

+ Sixty-one percent state they have "become more interested in peace or social justice" (51 percent n-c).

+ Forty-two percent have "become involved in volunteer work in your community" (44 percent n-c).

+ Eighty-seven percent have "experienced feeling better about yourself."

+ Eighty-four percent say they are "more honest and open about yourself" (70 percent n-c).

+ Eighty-three percent say they have "more open and honest communication with other people."[1]

Wuthnow drew the following conclusions from this study:

> In sum, the small-group movement has been successful in attracting a relatively large segment of the American public into its ranks. Its members attend meetings frequently and over long periods of time. Most who have ever been involved are still involved. Current members express high levels of satisfaction with their groups. They feel cared for and supported. And they believe their groups function well.[2]

He added this observation about church-based small groups: "What is [clear] from the survey is that church-based groups are an effective means of keeping church members active, and perhaps even of activating nominal members."[3]

These findings are consistent with an earlier survey by the Gallup Organization in 1988 commissioned by then-Presiding Bishop Edmond Browning and reported in the booklet *The Spiritual Health of the Episcopal Church*.[4] The Gallup Organization suggested that development in the following areas would further improve the spiritual health of the church:

+ Listening to people's remarkable religious experiences and spiritual journeys.

+ Encouraging evangelism and invitation.

+ Encouraging an exploration of new expressions of faith.

+ Encouraging a deepened prayer life.

+ Encouraging study of the Bible.

Then the research organization recommended a focus on small-group development: "Perhaps the best vehicle for carrying out the steps described—and for changing church life from the merely functional to the transformational—are small groups—groups that meet for Bible study, prayer, or special ministries."

Small groups can meet the need to:

1. Become open and vulnerable to each other, to become healed.

2. Deepen one's prayer life.

3. Study Scriptures and to bring the Bible into one's daily life in a meaningful way.

4. Test one's faith and to gain insight into such basic questions as: What is my relationship to God? Who is Jesus Christ and what does he mean to me?

5. Learn how to share one's faith with others in the group.

6. Become equipped to reach out to others outside the group and share one's faith.

7. Become empowered for social service and outreach.[5]

In more recent times writers and consultants on churches and church growth have emphasized the need for small groups. Diana Butler Bass has written of how small groups can help churches "re-tradition" ancient Christian practices for contemporary times.[6] Congregational development consultant Kennon Callahan makes small groups one of his twelve keys for church growth.[7] And the Natural Church Development model makes "holistic small groups" a key part of its platforms for development. Given such an emphasis on small groups in churches by so many, it is important that we take a look at the different kinds of small groups and the location of spiritual companionship groups within that range.

Varieties of Small Groups

Willow Creek, a megachurch that sees itself as a church of small groups, provides the following ways of classifying groups:[8]

Age/Stage Based—children, youth, singles, couples, families, men, women, etc.

Need Based—pastoral care and a community of support for people experiencing health or economic crisis, grief recovery, divorce, recovering from addictions, etc.

Task Based—service groups focused on meeting needs within the church (ushers, building and grounds, altar guild, vestry, choir, etc.) or in outreach responding to the needs in the world (food pantry, Heifer Project, Habitat for Humanity, etc.).

Interest Based—shared interest (Bible study, prayer, or other spiritual formation groups, movies, restaurant exploration, etc.) or common profession, skill, hobby, etc.

While this classification system is useful, I think it is helpful to supplement this by categorizing groups on two axes—whether the group is oriented on task/problem solving or support/guidance, and whether it primarily focuses on providing information/action or serves the formation/contemplative shaping of its members. This can be graphed as follows:

TASK/SUPPORT AND INFORMATION/FORMATION CONTINUUM

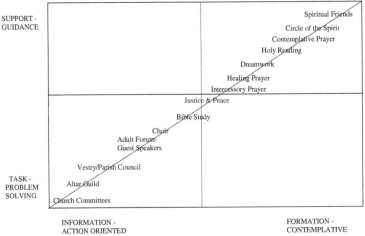

These are only intended as examples of different groups in a church, descriptive rather than prescriptive. Actual placement on a continuum could vary considerably depending on the particular purposes, process, and content of the group.

Daniel Prechtel 2008

The particular groups we will look at in detail in this book will be those that emphasize the formation/contemplative and support/guidance dimensions of group life, such as those listed closest to the upper right quadrant. This is not to diminish the importance of other groups, but to recognize that there are substantial differences among groups. These are spiritual companionship groups that are concerned about mutual support and spiritual guidance, desire spiritual formation of members, often engage in contemplative practices to help shape members' spiritual lives, and intentionally mediate opportunities for encountering the Divine Presence.

But first we will look at the backstory of how spiritual guidance has developed, especially in Christian traditions, and what has helped shape group spiritual companionship. For the Christian and Jewish traditions have much to share about divine interaction with humans.

Development of Traditions of Spiritual Guidance

Ancient Roots

Spiritual companionship and guidance have ancient, prehistoric roots. Our early human ancestors developed a capacity for recognizing a spiritual dimension to life, manifest by being in touch with a sense of wonder and mystery and an interest in investigating and interacting with the internal and external forces that influence and shape life. Traditional shamans, seers, oracles, prophets, priests, and sages are the ancestors of this art and ministry.

The Hebrew Scriptures

The Hebrew Scriptures reveal God's intimate interest and involvement in human history, desire for companionship with the created order, and intent to make divine guidance known in human affairs. God offers companionship and guidance on multiple levels, ranging from personal relationships to communities, peoples, nations, and globally.

In the Hebrew Scriptures we see various ways that God provided spiritual companionship and guidance. For example:

- Moses and the seventy elders (Num. 11:10–30) received a portion of God's spirit for leading and working with those on the Exodus journey in the wilderness.

- Ruth and Naomi ventured together back to Naomi's homeland. Ruth received her mother-in-law's mentoring (Book of Ruth), which has been understood as a prototype for spiritual friendship.

- Prophetic guilds or bands emerge in Scripture as early as the eleventh century BCE. Samuel was the leader of such a guild (1 Sam. 10:5; 19:20).

- The prophet-priest Samuel provided spiritual challenge and guidance to Israel, and at the insistence of the people, anointed King Saul (1 Sam. 9–13).

- Jonathan and David's friendship (1 Sam. 18:1–3) is viewed as a prototype of spiritual friendship.

- The prophet Nathan both counseled and challenged King David when he set up the killing of Bathsheba's husband (2 Sam. 12:1–15).

- The ninth-century BCE relationship between Elijah and Elisha gives us a glimpse of the mentor/disciple pattern of this prophetic tradition (1 Kings 19:16–21).

- The prophets of the sixth century BCE continued to provide spiritual counsel and challenge to royal courts and people during this tumultuous period of exile and return, as evidenced in the writings of the major and minor prophets such as Isaiah, Jeremiah, Micah, and Amos. Much of the challenge was related to unjust treatment of those who were socially and economically most vulnerable.

Christian New Testament

Christian tradition claims that God intimately dwells with us and calls us to be at one with God through Jesus Christ in the power of the Holy Spirit. The mystery of the Incarnation speaks of divine wisdom fully embracing human flesh and becoming one with humankind in Jesus of Nazareth.

Jesus in turn called together a small band of disciples to live intimately with him and one another. In that intimate context disciples were eventually formed into an apostolic band of Spirit-empowered people equipped to share the good news of God's love breaking through in Christ.

Early Christian writings such as Paul's letters, in 1 Corinthians 12:4–11, 28; Ephesians 4:11; and Romans 12:6–8, instruct the communities that the Holy Spirit disperses gifts (*charisms*) among the members for the benefit of the whole community of the faithful. Some of those gifts helped provide spiritual guidance and support for the community, such as the gifts of prophecy, the discernment of spirits, wisdom, knowledge, and pastoring.

Age of Martyrs

In the age of martyrs, the faith of Christian communities was tested by the threat of persecution—people risked their economic, social, and physical well-being in following Christ. Such testing during persecution entailed the formation of secret faith communities supporting their members, who when discovered were called upon to make a courageous witness to the reign of Christ in the face of a hostile empire. This period of time saw the development of *catechists,* who provided formation and instruction of those candidates (the *catechumens*) who were in preparation, sometimes for several years, before their baptismal initiation into the Christian community.

Desert Elders

By the fourth century the Christian religion had undergone a tremendous change. Emperor Constantine legalized Christian worship by the Edict of Milan in 313, and as its patron gave Christianity favored status in the Roman Empire. People began flooding into Christian churches when it became socially desirable to be identified with them. Now Christianity became marked by internal strife over theological issues. The testing of a vital spirituality was becoming more interiorly focused in the absence of general persecution and the dangers of a diluted civic religion. Some Christians moved away from the urban centers to the desert wilderness to seek God, confront their personal demons, attain purity of heart, and refine their spiritual lives.

This era marks the beginnings of the tradition of the desert elders, the ammas and abbas, the spiritual mothers and fathers who usually were solitaries living in the desert wildernesses of Egypt, Palestine, Arabia, and Persia. These abbas and ammas were sought out as spiritual guides by fellow anchorites (hermit monks) and visitors from the urban areas in their own quests for holiness. The era of the desert elders (especially from the fourth through sixth centuries, but beginning earlier with some anchorites such as St. Anthony) gave birth to a recognized tradition of seeking personal counsel from an experienced and mature spiritual guide.

The desert elders emphasized a simple spiritual rule of life, memorization and recitation of Scripture (especially the Psalms), silence and contemplation, discerning the source of thoughts, and fasting and other ascetical practices. A key goal was to become a well-ordered person, reflecting that one was made in the image of God (*imago Dei*). Although living separately, many of these early monks regularly gathered weekly for a common liturgy on a Saturday night or Sunday.

Many of the stories and counsels of these early spiritual directors were remembered and passed on by word of mouth, and eventually collected as the *Sayings (Apophthegmata) of the Desert Fathers.* Here are some examples of these sayings:

> A brother came to Scetis to visit Abba Moses and asked him for a word. The old man said to him, "Go, sit in your cell, and your cell will teach you everything."[9]

> A brother questioned an old man saying, "What good thing shall I do so that I may live?" The old man said, "God knows what is good.

I have heard it said that one of the Fathers asked Abba Nisterus the Great, the friend of Abba Anthony, and said to him, 'What good work is there that I could do?' He said to him, 'Are not all actions equal? Scripture says that Abraham was hospitable and God was with him. And David was humble, and God was with him. Elias loved interior peace and God was with him. So, do whatever you see your soul desires according to God and guard your heart.'"[10]

Abba Lot went to see Abba Joseph and said to him, "Abba, as far as I can I say my little office, I fast a little, I pray and meditate, I live in peace and as far as I can, I purify my thoughts. What else can I do?" Then the old man stood up and stretched his hands toward heaven. His fingers became like ten lamps of fire and he said to him, "If you will, you can become all flame."[11]

Amma Syncletica said, "In the beginning there are a great many battles and a good deal of suffering for those who are advancing towards God and afterwards, ineffable joy. It is like those who wish to light a fire; at first they are choked by the smoke and cry, and by this means obtain what they seek (as it is said: 'Our God is a consuming fire' [Heb. 12:29]): so we must also kindle the divine fire in ourselves through tears and hard work."[12]

Development of Monasticism

A further development from the desert experience was the growth of monasticism and the intentional Christian communal form of guidance shaped by a mutually agreed upon rule or *regula* (such as the fourth-century *Rule of Pachomius* and *Rules of St. Basil,* and the sixth-century *Rule of St. Benedict*), which members took upon themselves for the stability of the community and the spiritual well-being of the members. The monastic movement provided early and continuing emphasis on communal dimensions of spiritual guidance, as well as provided elders within the community for the spiritual direction of its members.

Great spiritual directors who arose from those monastic communities over the centuries included John Cassian, Aelred of Rievaulx (with his treatise *On Spiritual Friendship*), Bernard of Clairvaux, Catherine of Siena, and the Spanish Carmelite mystics John of the Cross and his own spiritual director, Teresa of Avila. Spiritual direction was also provided by members of the mendicant orders, including their great founders, Francis of Assisi and his sister Clare, who embraced "holy poverty" and identified with Jesus' suffering humanity, and Dominic, who emphasized preaching.

Women as Spiritual Mentors

Alongside the monastic orders there is a tradition in Christian practice of women exerting an influence on their families and being recognized as spiritual mentors and guides. Some of these great spiritual leaders include:

- Helena, mother of Emperor Constantine (third century)

- Macrina, sister of Basil the Great and Gregory of Nyssa (fourth century)

- Monica, mother of Augustine of Hippo (fourth century)

- Mary, sister of Pachomius (fourth century) and founder of women's monastic communities

- Scholastica, sister of Benedict (sixth century) and superior of a woman's monastic community.

Celtic *Anam Cara*
Soul Friendship

The Irish *anam chara* (soul friend) tradition predates Christianity. Usually, chieftains were accompanied by their counselors or druids at court. When Christian clerics and saints supplanted druids, they became voluntary soul friends/counselors and spiritual guides of the kings. Often the soul friend was a laywoman or layman.[13]

Besides Brigid (sixth century), two other Celtic women saints were known particularly for their guidance of souls—Íde (b. 480) and Samhthann (sixth century). St. Íde was known as the foster mother of the Irish saints and Brendan was said to be her chief foster child. Brendan and Columbanus confessed to women soul friends.[14]

Celtic spiritual guidance presents a tradition that is neither necessarily male nor clergy dominated. The soul friend was seen as an essential spiritual counselor and guide, and the saying attributed to Brigid became an established Celtic proverb: "Anyone without a soul-friend is a body without a head."[15]

Eastern Orthodox Spiritual Direction

The tradition of spiritual companionship can also be found in the Eastern church, as we see from this excerpt from *The Way of a Pilgrim,* a nineteenth-century journal of a Russian peasant journeying through Russia and seeking the guidance of the *starets* (spiritual director):

> [The *starets*] opened the book [*The Philokalia*], found the instruction
> by St. Simeon the new theologian, and read: "'Sit down alone and
> in silence. Lower your head, shut your eyes, breathe out gently, and

imagine yourself looking into your own heart. Carry your mind, that is, your thoughts, from your head to your heart. As you breathe out, say "Lord Jesus Christ, have mercy on me." Say it moving your lips gently, or simply say it in your mind. Try to put all other thoughts aside. Be calm, be patient, and repeat the process very frequently.'"... The *starets* sent me away with his blessing and told me that while learning the prayer I must always come back to him and tell him everything, making a very frank confession and report; for the inward process could not go on properly and successfully without the guidance of a teacher.[16]

This passage presents us with a short version of the Orthodox Jesus Prayer, which we will mention in discussion of contemplative prayer in chapter 3. Note that the *starets* takes on the role of confessor and spiritual teacher in this tradition.

Fourteenth-Century English Spiritual Directors

The fourteenth century gave England a special flowering of spiritual directors who wrote about prayer and mystical theology. They included:

* Anonymous, *The Cloud of Unknowing* and *The Book of Privy Counsel,* which provided guidance in prayer and other spiritual counsel

* Walter Hilton, *The Ladder of Perfection,* which was quite likely written for spiritual directors

* Julian of Norwich, who wrote *Revelations of Divine Love,* or *Showings,* and was an anchorite spiritual director whose directees included Margery Kempe.

Ignatian Spiritual Direction

Another historical element of spiritual guidance that influences present practices is the development of the Ignatian Spiritual Exercises in the sixteenth century. Ignatius of Loyola, the founder of the Society of Jesus (Jesuits), developed a systematic process for inner spiritual formation and commitment to serving Christ. This process included an intensive, extended retreat making use of Scripture, imagination, affect, and meditation guided by a spiritual director. The tools that Ignatius developed for the use of imagination and for considering the affective (feeling) dimension of our lives in the service of spiritual discernment and spiritual growth have been a lasting gift that continues to be adapted for use in current spiritual guidance practices.

Ignatius, with his companions, also developed practices for communal spiritual discernment (deliberations) that have had a lasting influence.

Pastoral-based Direction
in Anglican Tradition

Anglican spiritual direction has been strongly influenced by the sixteenth-century *Book of Common Prayer* (and later revisions)—the principal authorized liturgical and devotional resource shared by the clergy and parishioners. This tradition has emphasized the pastoral dimension of the clergy's care for their parishioners. For example, in the 1662 *Book of Common Prayer,* in the exhortation to Holy Communion, we find these words:

> And because it is requisite, that no man should come to the holy Communion, but with a full trust in God's mercy, and with a quiet conscience; therefore, if there be any of you, who by this means [personal confession and repentance to God] cannot quiet his own conscience herein, but requireth further comfort or counsel, let him come to me, or to some other discreet and learned Minister of God's Word, and open his grief; that by the ministry of God's holy Word he may receive the benefit of absolution, together with ghostly counsel and advice, to the quieting of his conscience, and avoiding of all scruple and doubtfulness.[17]

In that invitation to speak to a discreet priest and receive "ghostly counsel and advice" there is an implied intention that goes beyond legalistic concerns to that of a spiritual healing—of quieting the conscience and being freed from scruple or doubts.

Nicholas Ferrar and the Little Gidding community that flourished in seventeenth-century England was an early attempt to adapt Christian monastic practices to a lay community of families. A group of related families, about thirty people, shared a simple rule of prayer and worked under Deacon Nicholas Ferrar's leadership based on Scripture and the *Book of Common Prayer.*[18]

Quaker Guidance and
the Clearness Committee

The seventeenth century saw the birth of the Society of Friends (commonly called Quakers), a Protestant group that remains fiercely democratic and anti-authoritarian. Traditional meetings are marked by a contemplative silence where members look within for the inner Light, the source of any divine wisdom in Quaker spiritual tradition. The Clearness Committee developed as a small group of trusted Friends that gathers to help an individual or couple to discern God's direction when they are facing major life decisions (new job, relocating, getting married, etc.). Grounded in silent prayer, group members ask the kinds of questions that help clear away any interior clouds that prevent the focus person from discovering his or her true way.

The late Douglas Steere, a Quaker writer on prayer and spirituality, wrote what could well be considered a central tenet of contemporary spiritual direction: "To 'listen' another's soul into a condition of disclosure and discovery may be almost the greatest service that any human being ever performs for another."[19]

Wesleyan Small-Group Guidance

Another Protestant contributor to the communal dimension of spiritual guidance was the Methodist movement of the eighteenth century and the creation of a small-group system of spiritual nurture and guidance. The three groups in this system were called *classes, bands,* and the *select band.* There was a group for those new to Christian spiritual disciplines and instruction led by a mentor, a group for the various mentors of the classes, and a group for those who were the leaders. In contemporary practice this has given rise to small covenant groups among the Methodists, as well as evangelical megachurches organized as churches of small groups, where everyone has membership, from leaders to seekers, in a support or interest group.

Self-Help Groups

One of the major developments of the twentieth century has been the growth of Alcoholics Anonymous (AA) and related Twelve Step groups to provide peer support for people suffering from addiction processes in their lives or the lives of those to whom they are close. AA's origins in the 1930s came from the influence of the Oxford Group applied specifically to those members who struggled with alcoholism. The Twelve Steps developed as a spiritual path for sobriety and helping others. Among the early leaders influencing this movement was the Reverend Sam Shoemaker, an Episcopal priest and rector of Calvary Church in New York City, which was the United States headquarters of the Oxford Group. Bill Wilson was a member of that Oxford Group at Calvary Church, and Shoemaker helped him proofread *The Big Book* of Alcoholics Anonymous.

Since that time the meeting structure and Twelve Steps have been adapted to help people in their struggles with many other addictions or dependencies and to support family members or close friends of those who are fighting addictions. Having attended such meetings myself, as well as occasionally providing spiritual direction, pastoral, or confessional support for others, I can attest to the power of peer support both in meetings and with sponsors, the group wisdom that can emerge in meetings, and the efficacy of the Twelve Steps as a spiritual rule of life. More primary life-or-death spirituality goes on in those groups than nearly anywhere else I know.

Recent Developments
in Spiritual Direction

The late 1960s saw the beginning of a movement to reclaim the theological implications of divine immanence. Liturgical movement theology emphasized a baptismal ecclesiology in which baptism is the source of all ministry and ministry is centered on and offered by the laity. At the same time, Eastern religious teachers began to rise in popularity in the West, and people were hungry for direct spiritual encounters with the Divine, with competent guides into inner spiritual experience.

The mid-1970s to early 1980s saw an increasing demand for individual spiritual guidance and practices that would help bring a deeper consciousness of the presence of God in ordinary living—a movement out of the cloister and into the mainstream of Christian community. Many ecumenical training programs in spiritual direction have their beginnings during this time, alongside Roman Catholic spiritual direction training centers.

Since that time, ecumenically based training programs have proliferated, with a similar expansion of seminary programs that offer degrees related to spiritual direction. We have seen some developments in interfaith spiritual guidance training as well, and a rise in programs that provide formation in group spiritual direction and related group leadership. Spiritual Directors International, an umbrella organization started in 1990, has a membership of over fifteen thousand people across the world representing many faith traditions and approaches to spiritual direction. It now hosts annual conferences in both the United States and other parts of the world.[20]

A major shift in spiritual direction since the 1970s is a movement away from an emphasis on teaching and confession toward a focus on holy listening and sacred hospitality. Practitioners now are less directors, in the sense of providing directive programs for spiritual growth, and more of spiritual companions to persons on their own spiritual journey of self-discovery. Instead of assuming that we know what the person truly needs and that it is our responsibility to direct the person to meet that need, we become (to use Margaret Guenther's image) a "spiritual midwife," using holy listening and hospitality to assist the person in birthing their deeper relationship to the Divine Mystery.

Theological Foundations

The Christian spiritual tradition is broad, and the following theological foundations, while not universally agreed upon, arguably speak to why spiritual companionship groups can have an important role in spiritual development. Also, not all leaders, group members, or groups are going to have a Christian orientation. It is my hope that other faith traditions find parallels to some of these theological underpinnings that help illuminate spiritual dynamics that are important to them.

Incarnational Presence

In the Episcopal Church's *Book of Common Prayer* there is a startling question asked of those who are renewing their Baptismal Covenant: "Will you seek and serve Christ in all persons, loving your neighbor as yourself?"[21] The Hebrew and Christian Scriptures attest to God's presence with humanity. In the Christian gospels of Matthew and Luke the birth narratives show Jesus as God's desire to be at one with humanity, and in the Gospel of John the prologue speaks of the incarnation as the Word taking on flesh and dwelling among us. God takes on human flesh, becomes incarnated, in a particular culture and time with a particular person in Jesus of Nazareth. But just as unity between God and Jesus is stressed, so too is unity between Jesus and those he claims as his own (see Matthew 25:40). Recognizing the inner divine Presence is, of course, not restricted to Christian faith.[22] And so in spiritual companionship, to be present to another person is also to be present to the incarnated Presence in the other as well as in ourselves.

Immanence and Transcendence

God is the very ground of our being, a Presence that is indwelling as well as overarching all creation and the cosmos. One of the ways some Christian theologians try to speak of this sense of both divine immanence and transcendence is the word *panentheism* ("all in God"). God cannot be contained or limited to the whole of creation, but neither is anything outside of God's presence.[23] In a spiritual companionship group we will draw upon and trust in that sense of divine immanence, the sacred presence of the Divine within the group, and yet have the humility to recognize that this presence is a gift to us and remember that God is always beyond us, transcendent, too.

Community

From the Jewish and Christian perspective, we human beings are made to be in community. In the ancient creation story, after the creation of a human being and all other creatures, God declares, "It is not good that *adam* [the human being] should be alone" (Gen. 2:18). We are made to be in relationship with other human beings as well as with the rest of creation and God. That theme of community continues to develop in the Hebrew and Christian Scriptures. God is the God of *peoples* and *nations* and not just particular individuals in isolation. God's actions in human history formed and shaped a particular people, Israel, to become a light to all nations.

Jesus called together a band of disciples to live together in community and to follow him in his life and ministry. Others were attracted to Jesus, and the circle of disciples widened. From that original community of Jesus' followers, with the Holy Spirit's empowerment, the church community—the *ecclesia*—was born and flourished. A key attribute of this early church was its emphasis on *koinonia*—Christian fellowship, proclamation of the Good News, and communion.

In such texts as John 14–17, where Jesus prepares the disciples to share in the relationship with him and the Father through the Spirit, we get a picture of the nature of divinity as an intimate relationship of love. Trinitarian theology developed that theme, especially in the Eastern Orthodox concept of *perichoresis,* which suggests an inter-penetrating dance-like movement. In that view, the persons of the Trinity are in a perfect dance of mutuality and love that invites creation to join in. God is the original community that invites us into the ever-expanding divine communion of love and unity.

Community, therefore, is a key consideration in small-group formation for spiritual companionship. We are meant to be in communion with one another and with God. Thus to participate in building a deep sense of community is a sacred activity.

Covenant

Integral to any consideration of community is the biblical notion of a relationship built on divine promise and responsibility. The idea of covenant underwent a change among the people of Israel over time, from a contractual relationship between a less powerful person or people and a lord, where the lesser served the stronger and the stronger offered protection, to a promised relationship bound by God's love and faithfulness (*chesed*). There are various covenants mentioned in Scripture between God and humans: the covenants with Noah and with Abraham, which were renewed with Isaac and Jacob; the covenant with Moses and the people of Israel on Mount Sinai; the covenant with King David and his descendants; and the "new covenant" established through Jesus, sacramentally celebrated in the Holy Eucharist and in Holy Baptism. God established a covenant with Noah with the sign of the rainbow and a promise that God would never again flood the whole earth. For their part, Noah and his descendants were to abstain from consuming blood (Gen. 9). In the Abrahamic covenant God promised Abram (later named Abraham) a multitude of descendants and a new land as he followed God's call in his old age (Gen. 15). God established a covenant with Israel as Moses received the Ten Commandments on Mount Sinai and regulated worship and the practices of that nation (Exod. 19-23). God established a covenant with David and his offspring to establish a kingdom forever (2 Sam. 7). In the Christian Scriptures Jesus became the way for a new covenantal relationship with God, which later became extended to non-Jewish peoples through Paul's ministry. Interestingly, in the controversy over admission of Gentiles to this new faith, the Council of Jerusalem recalls God's covenant with Noah as the basis of restrictions on Gentile converts (Acts 15:28–29), forgoing the demand for circumcision and adherence to Jewish laws.

So another key dimension of a spiritual companionship group is to recognize that we promise something important to each other and to God in our gathering together. There should be a sense of promised faithfulness and lovingkindness in the relationships we enter into, that we hold ourselves accountable to each other for the spiritual well-being of the group and its members, and that we invite and seek God's presence in our midst.

Peace

Shalom in the Hebrew, or *eirene* in the Greek, is the scriptural concept of peace that is a gift of God, conveying well-being, unity, completeness, and wholeness. This sense of peace is not essentially individual—in its fullness it is communal. For example, Psalm 29:11 expresses this couplet: "May the LORD give strength to his people! / May the LORD bless his people with peace!" In Isaiah 54:9–10 peace is a covenanted relationship between God and the people, with an allusion to God's covenant with Noah. In Christian theology Jesus is the peace of God. His actions of healing and forgiveness of sins become signs of God's peace and God's realm breaking through in human experience.

In a spiritual companionship group we can look with expectancy toward the gift of this rich sense of peace. Although we cannot make or create this peace, we can be open to receiving this gift from God. It is not so much a moment or a static state of being as it is a movement toward a greater sense of wholeness, unity, or healing.

Spiritual Hospitality

The ancient code of the desert was and is to provide hospitality to strangers who are in need. The biblical story of Abraham and Sarah entertaining the three mysterious men under the oak trees of Mamre is archetypal of that rule (Gen. 18). In that story the Lord takes the form of three men and visits Abraham. Abraham runs to Sarah and asks her to provide a meal for them. In the unfolding of the story, Abraham and Sarah are promised that they will have a son. The hospitality that was shown to the strangers results in a promise of blessing.

The sixth-century *Rule of St. Benedict,* the foundation for Western Christian monasticism, insists that all visitors to the monastery are to be welcomed as Christ: "All guests who present themselves are to be welcomed as Christ, who said: 'I was a stranger and you welcomed me.'"[24] I maintain that spiritual hospitality is absolutely central to spiritual companionship groups. In my formation programs I offer students these thoughts at the beginning of their formation as group and retreat leaders:

> Spiritual hospitality is what we can offer each other. It is a way of respecting each other as companions on a journey toward wholeness and regarding each other as already bearing the sacred Presence within. To have a hospitable spirit is to be open to receiving the gifts *from* others as well as freely offering our gifts *to* others. It is also to accept the limitations of the other as part of his or her uniqueness, as well as to recognize and humbly accept our own limitations as part of a complex blend of attributes that shape who we are. Together we discover anew the truth that a greater wholeness grows out of our mutual sharing of gifts and acceptance of limitations. Spiritual hospitality aims to receive others without judgment or a need to convert or apply tests of doctrinal correctness. While respecting our critical thinking abilities and the traditions that have given shape and meaning to our lives, an approach of spiritual hospitality also invites us to be open to new and creative ways in which the Mystery can visit us and dwell in our midst. In that very openness to the divine Presence, and to each other, we will provide profound assistance to each other, and growth and change will occur.

> I am grounded in the Christian spiritual tradition and gratefully find much meaning and guidance from this great faith tradition, as well as from my denominational affiliation and service in the Church. And yet, as I practice spiritual hospitality I do not confine the working of the Spirit to any particular religious or faith tradition or make exclusive claims for God's favor on behalf of anyone. Instead, in a basic stance of spiritual hospitality I discover an inner eagerness to explore how other people experience the sacredness in life and how

that might enrich my own faith and life, even as at times it will challenge me. I also explore how I might respectfully share my own spiritual experience and perspective on a dynamic truth that is always far greater than myself.

This is not a program on methods of Christian evangelism, yet the deepest kind of relational evangelism may be discernible in our relationship together and in our mutual discovery of the Holy in our midst. The focus of this program is on creating an environment defined by respectful sacred hospitality, the nurture of a group contemplative awareness, and the mutual discovery and enjoyment of the God that is already present within and among us, and in this wonderful world we have inherited and in which we live as part of the Holy Mystery's unfolding creative love.[25]

Spiritual Discernment

We have to make a multitude of choices and decisions in our lives. Most of these decisions are fairly low-level concerns, but there are also many significant issues that we face that will have a major impact on us and others who are in our network of relationships. Our values, the quality of our lives, our self-understanding and the image we have of ourselves, strong emotions of anxiety or fear and hopes and desires are likely to emerge. All of this and more will be what we may need to consider in some situations that life brings us. We need people in our lives who can assist us in sorting through the various forces that influence our decisions and path in life.

Spiritual discernment means to disclose, uncover, or discriminate between the forces underlying an issue or choice of directions and to seek as much clarity as possible as to what path or direction God would have for the individual or community. A spiritual companionship group can partner with us in our desire to discern the most authentic path or choice. Our spiritual companions can help us listen deeply to our truest selves, our inner wisdom, and the invitations of the Divine.

Seeking divine wisdom in life choices is at the core of many spiritual traditions. It certainly shows up in many passages in the Hebrew and Christian Scriptures. Paul, in his letter to the young church in Rome, writes:

> I appeal to you therefore, brothers and sisters, by the mercies of God, to present your bodies as a living sacrifice, holy and acceptable to God, which is your spiritual worship. Do not be conformed to this world, but be transformed by the renewing of your minds, so that you may discern what is the will of God—what is good and acceptable and perfect. (Rom. 12:1–2)

Often the best assistance our spiritual companions can give is asking questions that encourage deeper exploration of our values and sense of truth rather than offering opinions. We do not need to carry the responsibility for others' decisions, but we can help them explore the issues, concerns, and desires that are part of decision-making. We will explore assisting companions in their discernment work in more detail when we look at the *Spiritual Friends* group in chapter 4. But we should expect that issues for spiritual discernment will emerge in any form of ongoing spiritual companionship group simply because people are intentional about living their lives in ways that are more deeply connected with the Spirit and their inner truth.

Transformation
The passage from Paul's letter to the community in Rome quoted above points to the expectation that active spiritual life is transformative. Encountering the Divine can reorient us, empowering us to see things from a different perspective, and equipping us to engage people and the world around us with an authenticity that draws wisdom from the wellspring of life, the source of creativity. Some traditions call this *enlightenment*; others speak of *conversion* or *metanoia;* terms like *purgative, illuminative,* and *unitive states* are also used, or some other names. Spiritual traditions may use different languages for this aspiration, but all attest to the transformative nature of our relationship with God or ultimate reality.

Spiritual companionship groups can provide the matrix, the sacred container, for that transformation to occur. We are not talking about a one-time event; while a profound shift can happen to a group member in a single meeting that sets that person on a new path, for most of us the transformative work is ongoing and lifelong. Even those who have had a born-again experience best benefit from openness to ongoing conversion, a spiritual suppleness and willingness to follow the Spirit's lead in the present and into their future. A companionship group can support its members in that ongoing desire for growth and spiritual change while providing a stable, loving environment within which that work can happen.

It is important to recognize that it is not the leader or the members of the group who are directly responsible for the spiritual transformation of its members. That is the work of the Divine, mysteriously present in our midst. The group helps by providing the opportunity, the sacred environment for that transformation to occur. But it is only God who does that deep work. We are not to try to force change in anyone, but rather we are to do that radical work of trusting that the true source of life and creativity will bring about the changes that are called for when the person is truly ready.

Mission and Service

The spiritual life is a two-way journey, moving both inward and outward. We attend to our interior life seeking new healing, wholeness, empowerment, and personal integration built on a deeper relationship with the indwelling divine Spirit. But as we discover the compassion of God acting within us to bring about new wholeness and wisdom and understanding, inevitably we will want to move out with compassion beyond ourselves.

In a video I saw many years ago, Ram Dass described a scene in India where an old Hindu holy woman was singing a love song to the Divine while others were busy passing out bread to all those who were in need. We need both worship and compassion for others. That scene is not so different from the Christian faith community experiencing and proclaiming God's love through Jesus Christ as the faithful are fed with the holy bread and wine of Eucharist. So too, the community advocates on behalf of, and in solidarity with, the hungry, homeless, and marginalized, and Christian members offer themselves in service. Or a Jewish *mitzvah* of visiting the sick or some other act of human kindness is initiated in faithful and loving response to God's commandments. Compassion flows from the deep core of our humanity as it is touched by divine mercy and lovingkindness.

Psycho-Spiritual Foundations

Besides the theological underpinnings of these kinds of groups, there are important psycho-spiritual dimensions that we should discuss as part of the foundational dynamics of a spiritual companionship group and its leadership. These foundations are easier to understand across religious traditions, or with those who are not oriented to a formal tradition.

Contemplative Awareness

Cultivating an awareness that we are always in the presence of the Holy One is a central aspect of the spiritual life. *Holy listening* is a term Margaret Guenther has made popular in spiritual direction circles for the way a director attends to the directee and the Spirit. The Christian contemplative tradition urges practicing silence, openness, alertness, self-emptying, and humility. In his magnificent study of a contemplative psychology in *Will and Spirit,* the late psychiatrist-turned-spiritual guide Gerald May wrote of having a stance of "willingness" over and against one of "willfulness." Much more will be said about contemplative awareness practices in chapter 3, when we look at a model of contemplative prayer.

What I emphasize now is that the leader of spiritual companionship groups should be disciplined about cultivating his or her personal openness to God in the midst of regular living. We cannot provide an environment for this in a group setting without first and always being attentive to our own lived experience of contemplative practice and growing awareness. Bernard of Clairvaux, a twelfth-century monastic leader, criticized those who were not sufficiently attentive to their own spiritual well-being but were rushing to the spiritual care of others. He contrasted being a "canal" with being a "reservoir" of God's grace:

> The canal simultaneously pours out what it receives; the reservoir retains the water till it is filled, then discharges the overflow without loss to itself. . . . Today there are many in the church who act like canals, the reservoirs are far too rare. So urgent is the charity of those through whom the streams of heavenly doctrine flow to us, that they want to pour it forth before they have been filled; they are more ready to speak than to listen, impatient to teach what they have not grasped, and full of presumption to govern others while they know not how to govern themselves. . . . You must imitate this process. First be filled, and then control the outpouring.[26]

Without getting caught up in Bernard's meaning of "heavenly doctrine," if we attend to our own openness to the presence of the Holy One in our lives and are receptive to the loving and empowering grace of that primary relationship, then we will be better equipped to facilitate a group that invites others into their own awareness of the Source. We can all drink from that stream and be filled. But first we ourselves need to receive, and to know what it is like to live out of that reservoir of grace. Our quiet, practiced centeredness in God will greatly affect the group. We do not need to be masters of contemplative practice (ultimately it is a gift we cannot *make* happen anyway), but we should be attentive to cultivating that awareness ourselves as well as encouraging it in others.

Dimensions of Spiritual Experience and Spiritual Pathways

We all have capacities for engaging spiritual life, but we are not all the same in the ways we access those capacities. We may speak of people being drawn to different spiritual paths, or having different personalities that engage spiritual life in differing ways. Corinne Ware, in her book *Discover Your Spiritual Type,*[27] and others before her have introduced a typology of spiritual paths based on graphing two different capacities as polarities. One polarity is our ability to use our minds (the speculative way of engaging spiritual life) or using our feelings and emotions (the affective dimension of engaging spiritual life). Another polarity that shows up in spiritual traditions is approaching God as knowable (*kataphatic*) or as the Divine Mystery who is unable to be contained by our knowing (*apophatic*). From these different poles of experience, Ware gives names to four spiritual paths. The first is the *head path* (speculative–kataphatic), which emphasizes thoughtful order and a reasonable faith, use of Scripture for knowledge about the divine-human relationship, theological inquiry, and structured worship. Next is the *heart path* (affective–kataphatic), which focuses on divine actions

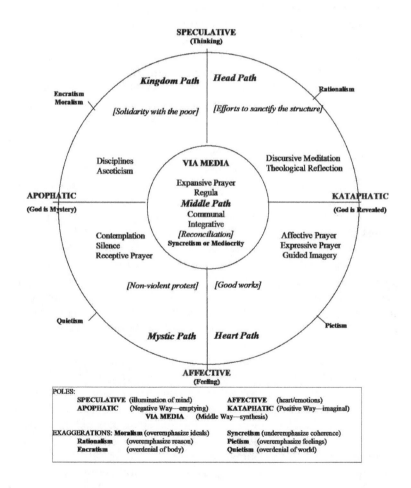

Spiritual Paths and the Landscape of Prayer   (D. Prechtel, 4/00)

Quadrants by Urban T. Holmes, Social components by Rachael Hosmer
Quadrant path names by Corinne Ware, Via Media component by Dan Prechtel

SPECULATIVE
(Thinking)

Kingdom Path   Head Path

Encratism
Moralism

Rationalism

[Solidarity with the poor]   *[Efforts to sanctify the structure]*

Disciplines
Asceticism

VIA MEDIA

Discursive Meditation
Theological Reflection

APOPHATIC
(God is Mystery)

Expansive Prayer
Regula
Middle Path
Communal
Integrative
[Reconciliation]
Syncretism or Mediocrity

KATAPHATIC
(God is Revealed)

Contemplation
Silence
Receptive Prayer

Affective Prayer
Expressive Prayer
Guided Imagery

[Non-violent protest]   *[Good works]*

Quietism

Pietism

Mystic Path   Heart Path

AFFECTIVE
(Feeling)

POLES:

SPECULATIVE	(illumination of mind)	AFFECTIVE (heart/emotions)
APOPHATIC	(Negative Way—emptying)	KATAPHATIC (Positive Way—imaginal)
	VIA MEDIA (Middle Way—synthesis)	

EXAGGERATIONS: Moralism (overemphasize ideals)   Syncretism (underemphasize coherence)
Rationalism   (overemphasize reason)   Pietism   (overemphasize feelings)
Encratism   (overdenial of body)   Quietism (overdenial of world)

27

through personal relationships, use of imagination in meditation, expressive and artistic forms of prayer, and a personal relationship with the Divine. Ware's third path is the *mystic path* (affective–apophatic), valuing silence, contemplation, imageless or simple repetitive prayer, and being present to the Mystery of God. The fourth path is the *kingdom path* (speculative–apophatic), which focuses on prophetic justice and moral vision, with spiritual disciplines in the service of discerning God's kingdom. There is a fifth middle-way path, or *via media,* that has access to the other paths or dimensions of the spiritual landscape. That middle way is integrative in nature and values practices like developing a spiritual rule of life, praying with Scripture by *lectio divina,* and seeking reconciliation.[28]

Each path expresses a concern for justice and compassion in the world. In a presentation she gave at Seabury-Western Theological Seminary in the early 1980s, Sister Rachel Hosmer, O.S.H., suggested examples of how this might play out. People operating from a head path might work for social change, like lobbying for new legislation and other efforts to sanctify the system. Heart path folk may wish to serve in soup kitchens and other forms of direct service to the poor. Mystics may wish to participate in nonviolent demonstrations. And kingdom path people may be the prophetic voices articulating movements in solidarity with the poor. I would add that the middle way values reconciliation activities, such as mediation dialogues between parties. Of course these are only a few examples; there are many other ways people may engage justice and compassion from these different spiritual paths.

It should be noted that a path also can become distorted. The head path might turn into rationalism, overemphasizing reason. The heart path could turn into a type of pietism that overemphasizes feelings and equates those emotions with faith. The mystic path could be turned into quietism or isolation, losing touch with community. The kingdom path could turn moralistic, or overly suspicious of the body (encratism), and excessively mortify the flesh. The middle way could become syncretistic and fail to have a firm and cohesive theological foundation, or succumb to an "anything-goes" attitude without sufficient convictions and end up in fence-sitting mediocrity. All of those are distortions of the gifts of the paths.

A classic model of understanding spiritual paths, articulated by Baron Friedrich Von Hügel in the early twentieth century, as well as by others, is the "Three Ways" of purgative, illuminative, and unitive states of prayer. The purgative way focuses on cleansing from sin and seeks purity of heart. Practices of this way include self-examination, confession of sin and the sacrament of reconciliation of a penitent, fasting, and prayer vigils. In the purgative way we value the rules and laws that help school us in right living, as we strive to keep the Ten Commandments (Exod. 20:1–17, Deut. 5:6–21), and seek to live according to Jesus' Summary of the Law (Luke 10:25–28) and his new commandment to love one another as he has loved us (John 15:12). The illuminative way brings us into deeper relationship with Christ and provides light to our living through practices such as Scripture study, especially *lectio divina* and other devotional ways of engaging Scripture, and meditating on the life of Christ. In this state we are focused on learning about the saints and teachings of the church, and on ministering as Spirit-empowered and gifted members of the body of Christ. The unitive way moves us to a deeper identification with Christ/God, as we seek to operate from the true self where the Spirit abides; the prayer practice in this way is often contemplative. Participation in the church's sacraments of Baptism and Holy Eucharist particularly reflect this unitive dimension. Within the Three Ways typology is the idea of stages of progression *within* a way by the practitioner: from novice, to proficient, to perfect.

Another understanding of spiritual paths has been articulated by Tilden Edwards in his book on recovering spiritual direction, *Spiritual Friend*.[29] This is a fourfold typology that has some correlation with Ware's typology. "The Way of Knowing" is a spiritual path in pursuit of truth, with two sub-types: analytic knowing and intuitive knowing. Analytic knowing pursues the truth through reason like Ware's head path, whereas intuitive knowing uses awareness like Ware's mystic path. The second way is "The Way of Action," and pursues personal and collective moral good and care for the world. The third way is "The Way of Prayer and Adoration," and pursues the path of beauty. The fourth way in this typology is "Fighting-It-All-the-Way," and is the iconoclastic way that seeks the God behind all the masks. Like Ware's typology, these all have positive sides but can also have their shadows.

The contemporary writer, teacher, and interfaith spiritual guide John R. Mabry suggests a different typology in *Faith Styles*. He proposes a primary triangle of Ethical Humanists–Traditional Believers–Spiritual Eclectics and a secondary triangle, which fits between the primary faith styles, of Jack Believers–Liberal Believers–Religious Agnostics.[30] His typological categories of faith styles stretch us to consider the spiritual dimension present in a greater range of belief systems than traditional religious thinking generally acknowledges. His work is particularly useful for an interfaith perspective, and his suggestions about the challenges and compatibility of the spiritual director's own style when engaged in guiding those of a different style are valuable.

There are certainly many ways of understanding how personality interfaces with spiritual traditions and prayer paths. Much work has been done in this area, as for example in the Myers-Briggs Personality Types and in the Enneagram, which describe different ways of understanding how personality affects spiritual life. Another consideration of how personality characteristics interface with spiritual life and practices is the current work being done based on Howard Gardner's theory of multiple intelligences. Kent Groff suggests how Gardner's seven categories of intelligence—linguistic, logical-mathematical, spatial, musical, kinesthetic, interpersonal, and intrapersonal—might affect the way a person understands and engages spiritual life.[31] There also has been much valuable work done in this area based on developmental psychology and its implications for faith and spiritual life stages and capacities, such as the contributions of James Fowler, Robert Kegan, and Elizabeth Liebert.[32]

In spiritual companionship with individuals or groups we do well to take into consideration the rich variety of personalities, experiences that have given shape to people's spiritual lives, and what spiritual dimensions or paths they are particularly attracted to when suggesting what resources of prayer and practice may benefit them. Again, we are not all the same, and yet others in the past and the present have walked similar paths and territory in the landscape of spirituality and in the way we seek, encounter, and attempt to understand the Divine.

All of this has implications for leading a spiritual companionship group or a group retreat. Members are likely to understand their spiritual lives in different ways. They will have different capacities and interests and modes of engaging spiritual practices. So it will be important to recognize the diversity within the group and allow for multiple ways to help members explore spiritual life. A one-size-fits-all approach rarely works for every member of the group.

Windows to Awareness

Spiritual companionship groups provide windows to awareness of the spiritual dimension to our lives, to the movements of the Spirit within and around us, and help us recognize factors that affect our living with spiritual depth and intentionality. Such groups can illuminate our inner reality and help us navigate toward greater wholeness.

The late Morton Kelsey, an Episcopal priest and professor at the University of Notre Dame, studied under Carl G. Jung and wrote many groundbreaking books that offered insights from depth psychology in the field of spirituality. One graph that Kelsey provided in several of his books looks like an iceberg lying on its side.[33] The smallest tip of human awareness is "consciousness" in the physical world. The rest of the iceberg (my word) is in the realm of the "psychoid or spiritual world" (his words). The area next to consciousness and a wider field, he identified as the realm of "memory." The next wider dimension he identified as the realm of "personal unconscious." Then there is a vast realm of what he called the "soul or psyche." It is composed of the "personal collective unconscious," which includes the internal unconscious influence and operation of the archetypes. That realm of soul is also influenced by forces that may be thought of as external to us: "psychic experience," "clear communication" (profound, intuitive knowledge that seems to come from beyond us), "numinous experience" (encounters with spiritual presences such as angelic and demonic beings and God, and other encounters with the holy), and what he called experiences of "visionary overview," where we might get a glimpse of some vast and profound truth that puts our life in a whole new perspective. All of these areas can be explored with the help of psychotherapists, spiritual directors, or some forms of spiritual companionship groups.

Katherine Marie Dyckman, S.N.J.M., and L. Patrick Carroll, S.J., presented a Johari window that graphed different areas of spiritual awareness in their book on spiritual direction, *Inviting the Mystic, Supporting the Prophet.*[34] There are four quadrants of awareness in this window. Two contain information known to the person, and two quadrants contain material that the person does not know about him or herself. Two quadrants have information that others know about the person, and two have information unknown to others.

Only one part of ourselves is generally shared, known by ourselves and others, and that area Dyckman and Carroll call the "Arena of Free Activity." The other areas are either unknown by ourselves, or by most others, or by both ourselves and others. The challenge is to expand the window of shared knowledge by inviting certain others that we trust into those areas. Companionship groups can serve us well by offering us a safe and respectful environment for exploring those other areas that we either keep to ourselves out of wounding, shame, or fear ("Secret Self"), or that we do not know about ourselves unless others reflect back to us what they see ("Blind Side"); or that is so deep (Kelsey's "personal unconscious" and "personal collective unconscious") that we are unaware of that part of ourselves unless we engage in such guided work as dreamwork, guided imagery meditations, and sacramental rituals ("Subconscious and Unconscious"). But in working with Dyckman and Carroll's window it became apparent to me that there are similar dimensions operative in groups themselves. So I have developed a Johari window to represent group awareness, shown on the following page.

A WINDOW FOR GROUP SPIRITUAL SELF-AWARENESS

	GROUP KNOWS ABOUT ITSELF	GROUP DOESN'T KNOW ABOUT ITSELF
OTHERS KNOW ABOUT GROUP	*Openness to Public Disclosure* • Mission/Purpose Statement • Descriptions of "what we do" • Invitations for sessions open to guests and visitors • Varying levels of trust and intimacy needs • External service to others • Degree of "open" stance	*The Blind Side/Shadow* • Group projections • Unexplored assumptions • Implicit group myths • Unrecognized gifts • Unconscious resistance tactics; such as dependency, fight/flight, pairing • Help from outsiders, such as facilitator, consultant, spiritual director to the group can increase group's ability to become aware of group dynamics, gifts, wounds.

OTHERS
 	
DON'T
 	
KNOW
 	
ABOUT
 	
GROUP
	The Hidden Identity
	
	• "Ingroup-Outgroup"
	• Initiatory stages
	• Insider's information
	• Needs for confidentiality
	• Degree of "closed" stance
	• Shamed activity or traumas from past needing healing
	• Occult or cult-type environment
	• Help from outsiders such as facilitator, consultant, spiritual director to group can help with group healing and appropriate levels of disclosure to others
		Realm of Mystery
		
		• Mystery of the group's collective unconscious known only to God.
		• Often requires competent guides to help probe these depths revealed in:
		   dream symbols on communal
		     level of meaning,
		   guided imagery meditations,
		   family & cultural roots,
		   discerning the spirit of the group
		• Rituals, sacraments, and symbols can speak to this dimension
		• Communal spiritual discernment practices

There are things the group knows about itself and chooses to share freely that I have named "Openness to Public Disclosure." Things like mission or purpose statements and descriptions about the group's activities and history tell the public about the group and its aspirations. Meetings that are open to visitors and guests help provide public accountability and potential growth in membership. If the group performs services to or for the community beyond itself, that becomes part of the shared arena of knowledge about the group. As with individuals, a group makes choices about how much it will share beyond itself and what are the boundary needs of disclosure. An AA group or other spiritual companionship group needs to maintain a certain degree of confidentiality in order to develop trust and encourage open and honest sharing among group members. That requires some degree of closed stance. But sometimes guests are invited and asked not to share with others outside the group what is said, although members are free to share with the public what the group means to them or how the group has affected them.

That need for appropriate confidentiality or a need for membership initiation also means there is a hidden identity to the group's life to varying degrees. In spiritual companionship groups we may find that it is difficult incorporating new members into a group that has been profoundly shaped by shared experiences that have occurred over time. Bringing in new members so that they are not overwhelmed by the level of intimacy that has been built may require the group to divide and offer some experienced members as leaders of a new group composed of mostly new members. Other groups might have periodic times where there is a formal closing with an opportunity for some members to end their time with the group and for new members to join, effectively creating a new group.

Although many groups have a healthy hidden identity, there are times when wounding, shaming, or other actions require interventions. Churches can suffer deeply because of sexual misconduct or active alcoholism by a pastor, and are rendered toxic until a consultant works with the congregation on steps toward recovery of health. A group can be paralyzed because of a member's bullying behavior when the leader and other members do not know how to confront the behavior. Someone from the outside might provide guidance and support to help the group appropriately deal with the concern. The group leader might participate in a colleague group for peer supervision and consultation that can help the leader reflect on the situation and possible actions.

There is likely to be a "Blind or Shadow Side" to the group that it is not aware of unless someone from outside or a skilled observer can reflect what he or she sees back to the group members. A group may project some of its own unwanted behavior and attitudes onto the outside world. The group may be unaware of or discount its gifts, or it may have norms and myths and assumptions it operates out of unconsciously that need to be recognized and explored. It may unconsciously resist doing its work by pairing activity, or forming a dependency upon the leader, or resisting change by fight-flight behavior. In all of this a consultant, spiritual guide, or skilled facilitator may help the group to expand its knowledge of itself and grow in its health and giftedness. A colleague group may help the leader by opening up new understandings and consequently new self-awareness for the group.

And, like the amazing depths of our psyche that are unknown to ourselves and others, there is a side to the group that is the "Realm of Mystery"—the group's collective unconscious and its deep hidden interactions with the spiritual realm. Knowledge and wisdom within this realm can emerge through such avenues as group discernment practices, group dreamwork, prayer, imagery meditations, and awareness exercises led by a competent spiritual guide from within the group as leader/facilitator or outside the group as a consultant.

This chapter has provided a great deal of foundational material to absorb. However, a group spiritual director or leader of a spiritual companionship group should be aware that these kinds of groups emerge in our present time from a past that is rich in theological meaning and history. There are profound spiritual and psychological dynamics at work in these groups that affect the members and the life of the group.

With this broad historical, theological, and psycho-spiritual context for our work as a group spiritual director, we can turn our attention to elements and considerations that are common to spiritual companionship groups.

chapter two

Essentials of Spiritual Companionship Groups

A WIDE RANGE of different models for small groups for spiritual companionship can be found today, and over the next several chapters we will look at ten of these companionship group models, as well as one model for group leader peer supervision. Hopefully these models will not only serve the most commonly shared group needs of the people who join them, but will also provide templates for designing other models that will be able to meet specific needs for a particular context. There are common components to this diverse array of groups, including *purpose, time,* suitable *group size,* and *structure.*

In this chapter we will look at each of these core elements in turn, followed by a more detailed discussion of what the basic group structure or design might look like in practice.

Core Elements

Purpose

The overarching purpose to these groups is identified by their name: *spiritual companionship groups.* Although the focus will vary, all of these groups have as central goals:

- To provide members with a healthy community for mutual emotional and spiritual support in their daily lives.

- To enable members to deepen their spiritual lives by sharing a common spiritual focus, the richness of peer perspectives and experiences, and mutual spiritual support.

- To provide an environment that invites and affirms a contemplative[1] awareness of the presence of God in our midst.

Thus a spiritual companionship small group seeks to establish an environment of spiritual hospitality where members give each other the freedom and safety to explore their inner truths, honor their desire to grow in their relationship to God, and build healthy relationships with others. Members offer mutual support as a small community committed to each other's emotional and relational well-being and spiritual development, providing ways to engage members in focused reflection and practice in their spiritual lives, and offering opportunities for discernment of God's leading in their lives. The methods will differ between group forms. But all of these groups provide spiritual companionship that is complementary to, or provides an alternative to, individual spiritual companionship (spiritual direction).

Time
In my experience, the amount of time allowed for each meeting of a spiritual companionship group varies greatly, from less than an hour to more than two or even three hours. In seminary and other small-group leadership training settings, these groups typically run for eighty to ninety minutes, with an additional twenty minutes allotted for a process review for learning purposes. Some of my church groups have been significantly shorter, fitting into a forty-minute time frame between Sunday worship services, while other groups less hampered by time constraints have run for two or more hours. If the group ranges in size between six to eight participants, I have found it is wise, if possible to plan for a companionship group to meet in session for ninety minutes. The biggest concern is to allow sufficient time for everyone to participate in check-in and sharing reflection times. The question of how frequently a group should meet has a number of variables, and we will look at that aspect more fully in chapter 7.

Group Size
The size of the group I have participated in has normally ranged from five to nine participants, including myself as facilitator or instructor or peer member; but some group meetings have held sessions where only two or three are gathered, and some have had upwards of twelve participants. We might recall that Jesus had a small inner core of three disciples (Peter, James, and John) and a primary group of twelve disciples that he most frequently interacted with during his ministry. Most of the writers on small groups indicate that twelve group members is the maximum size, and beyond that the group should subdivide into two new

groups. A group of less than four members is difficult to maintain due to the occasional absences of even the most committed members. With less than four it might be better to consider a one-to-one spiritual direction relationship with each member.

Structure

The other core element to be explored is structure—how the group organizes a session's inner movements. The structure is in a dynamic relationship with the other elements of purpose, time, and size. The components of the structure also are in a dynamic relationship with each other within the session—it is not a lockstep process, but rather more like movements in a dance or a symphony.

I have been involved with spiritual formation, mutual guidance, and support groups for about thirty years, and based on this experience I believe that such a group is best structured in the following way.

Basic Structure of a Spiritual Companionship Group

1. Simple Opening Ritual

2. Check-in Time

3. Group Focus

4. [Quiet Reflection/Journaling, Break]

5. Sharing Reflections and Responses

6. Process Review

7. Closing Ritual

There will be variations on this structure that the different models we will explore may help to identify. Also, time considerations and group size will affect the capacity to develop fully each of the movements. But most of the movements or structural components noted above will be a part of these small groups in their fullness. Let's amplify each of these movements or structural components. (Again, I suggest that the leader think of "movements" because of the dynamic flow that can happen in a group session.)

1. Simple Opening Ritual

Members should know that the group has begun at a particular moment in time, and hence we are no longer a collection of individuals—we belong to each other as group members. It is important therefore for a leader to call the group into being. Furthermore, the nature of this group is such that we recognize the time we spend gathered in the group session as sharing together in sacred time and space. Begin the group session with a simple ritual to mark the beginning of the group's time, and frame the session as sacred, spiritual time shared together. The leader may assist members in calling upon and welcoming the divine Presence, Christ's Spirit, Holy Wisdom, or other names for God, or use other language that points to the mystery of God's immanence in this sacred time and space—*making* this sacred time and space. How does this happen? Ritual moves us into an awareness of the holy and invites us to respond with the depths of our being, where holiness abides around and within us.

This group structure calls for a *simple* opening ritual. Most of these groups can go through this beginning movement in a minute or so. Ritual opening actions can include lighting a candle, ringing a chime or bell, offering a simple prayer, reading a short piece of Scripture or a poem, leading the group in a chant or song, playing some music, or even asking for a period of silence to gather ourselves as a group in the mystery of the Presence. The simple ritual gathers the individuals into the group and marks the time and space as reserved for spiritual companionship. Certainly, more elaborate ritual actions can be offered, especially when the actions lead into the next movement of the structure. For example, the leader might open the group by the simple ritual action of lighting a candle and then asking the group's members to pass the candle around, with whoever is holding the candle taking a few minutes to share whatever they wish about themselves as a way of checking in with the group. But the group does not need to begin with a lot of activity, and there is a contemplative dimension that simplicity can evoke that invites an open and reflectively prayerful atmosphere.

2. Check-in Time

A key feature of Christian community building is to create an environment of sacred hospitality and support. One of the ways this hospitality and support happens in spiritual companionship small groups is in the check-in time. I like to invite the group members to envision the circle (often the groups are formed in a circle) of members as framing the edge of a sacred bowl, a sacred container that can hold each of us and the concerns and joys and wonderments of our lives in loving regard and emotional care. In the midst of this sacred bowl is God's own Presence. Thus, whatever we bring to the group is held in loving and supportive care not only by our fellow companions in the group but by the Holy One. So during the check-in time I ask members to share as an offering into the sacred bowl and to trust that what is said is being graciously heard, received, and held by the members and by Christ's Presence. Thus, this is primarily a time for mutual listening. It is *not* intended for fixing or advice-giving. Little verbal response is needed or desirable. Crosstalk is not encouraged. *Anyone can choose to take a pass on sharing at the check-in or other times in the session.* The need for creating a safe and confidential environment is essential to building trust and a sense of mutual support of the members.

The leader can initiate the check-in time in many ways. Simplest, and often best, is to ask people to share briefly what they would like the group to know about how they are or what is happening in their life. Sometimes I will lead into check-in by asking group members to imagine the state of their "personal internal weather system." What kind of weather report would they give? Cloudy with high winds, or sunny and mild temperatures, or thunderstorm raging? Then they might follow up with a few thoughts about why this is so. Another question, which I credit to Dr. Ken Reid, who facilitated a long-term clergy support group and small diocesan group gatherings in which I participated, is: "What percentage of you is here and what percentage of you is somewhere else?" The check-in sharing is a good time to name those things or concerns that may hinder us from being fully present to each other. It becomes an opportunity to place those concerns or preoccupations into the sacred container to be respectfully, non-judgmentally received by the group's members and held by God through the duration of the session.

Typically the check-in time lasts only a short period for a newly composed group. But as the group builds a sense of trust in its members, its process, and its knowledge of members' life situations, this movement expands. Sometimes the leader will need to place more specific limits on the sharing in order to honor the other purposes of the group. A good way to discuss this is for the leader to bring this into the process review (of which more will be said later in this chapter). Use of a timer, passing a talking stick (or cross, or candle, etc.), asking people to keep their sharing to a few sentences, and other strategies can be employed to safeguard the purpose of this check-in time in relation to the rest of the group's work.

After everyone who chooses to share has done so, the leader might ask if anyone has anything else he or she wishes to add, or if anyone has a question for clarification of what a member has said. This can get tricky because it might result in excessive focus on a particular individual or situation. However, it can clarify or add critical information or provide an important supportive acknowledgment to a group member. The important thing is for the leader (with the group sharing responsibility) to watch that this does not get into problem solving, fixing, crosstalk, or other ways of distorting the purpose of the check-in period.

Sometimes a member of the group expresses a particularly weighty concern in the check-in time and there may be a feeling that in some way this needs more attention from the group. One way is to simply ask the person if there is anything that he or she needs from the group. Prayer for that concern and the member is an action the group can do with and on behalf of that member. I have seen such a specially offered prayer release the person who is carrying the concern, and the rest of the group's members, to continue to the next stage of the group's session. The community support for a member undergoing a tough time can also be expressed around the edges of the group's meetings—in a conversation during a break or after the meeting, in a note sent, in a promise of remembering the person in prayer between the sessions, or in other ways. In rare situations the group may decide to suspend their normal agenda and provide extended attention to the care needs of the member in distress.

3. Group Focus

A group has both its process (how does it do its work) and its content (what is the substance of its work). This movement in the group session presents the primary content of its spiritual work. Sometimes the ways into the content are heavily process-oriented—and that is often the case with spiritual companionship/formation groups. The content of such a group may vary widely depending on the focus of the group. We will look in chapters 3–7 at different models of groups and give details on what this third movement looks like for those particular groups. It is in this third movement of the group's session that the focus, and therefore content, will be most differentiated. But the group leader, or some other designated member, will bring the group into a shared focus and content. It may be using a passage of Scripture to leaven the members' thoughts and imaginations, or a dream that becomes the focus of exploring inner meaning and wisdom. Then again, perhaps it is a guided imagery meditation that leads members to rich inner worlds, or a particular social issue about which the members seek information and prayerful action in response. This movement that I am calling *group focus* is where the group begins exploring a particular subject and is given the tools to engage it fully.

However, as I mentioned earlier, this movement is also heavily process-driven in these kinds of groups. Let me illustrate this by contrasting two small groups that use Scripture as a primary means of reflection and discourse. A spiritual companionship group that I call a *Holy Reading* group (see chapter 3) is much more focused on God encountering us in the immediacy of the group session through Scripture than in the group's study of a passage in a book of the Bible for its historical background and form and structure. The *Holy Reading* group strongly emphasizes the *spiritual formation and contemplative insight* of its members, whereas a *Bible study* group is more likely to emphasize *religious information* about the Scripture passage. Both are valuable approaches in the overall formation of Christians, and many Bible study groups also provide mutual support, guidance, prayer, and spiritual formation of its members. However, the models we will look at, including the *Holy Reading* group, are more likely to emphasize supporting members' spiritual lives and providing a gentle environment for mutual guidance, rather than educational content or the accomplishment of tasks that primarily benefit the religious institution.

In summary, the leader moves members into engaging the particular focus or main content of the group's work together in this part of the session.

4. Quiet Reflection / Journaling / Break

This movement is in brackets in my initial list because it is only present or appropriate in some group processes. We will see that it is important to move the group into a period of silence where quiet reflection can occur with groups like the *Circle of the Spirit* and *Spiritual Friends* models. It can be beneficial in other groups as well. In planning a group design, be sure to consider whether group members are better served if they can spend some time in relaxed reflection and prayerful silence to gather their thoughts and feelings prior to a time of group sharing. Even if the particular group does not set aside a time for reflection or journaling as part of its process, members can be encouraged to maintain a journal outside group meeting time for making notes and reflections about their sessions and the themes, issues, and insights that emerge.

At some point the group may be ready for a brief break. Between major movements is a good time to do so. If check-in has been lengthy, a break before moving into the major content (focus) may be warranted. Another time that a break is not disruptive is at the end of a period of quiet reflection before the group regathers to share members' responses to the content or shared exercise.

5. Sharing Reflections and Responses

Engaging a subject of focus elicits members' responses, and ample time should be given for members to share what has arisen for them in the presentation or practice or spiritual exercise. This is a time for those who wish to share what associations they have with the subject, what this means for them, what questions they wish to explore more deeply, whether someone needs the group's support in some appropriate way, and what God might be inviting them to be or do. In chapter 7 we will look at some ground rules for a healthy group, but now is a good time to emphasize some things that help the group do its reflective sharing work:

♦ Practicing deep and respectful listening to one another is vitally important to the group.

♦ A nonjudgmental attitude among members is also important.

♦ It can be helpful if members speak out of their own experience and from their own perspective (using "I" statements), rather than impose general pronouncements on the members.

♦ Remembering that the group practices spiritual hospitality can allow for deep feelings to be expressed in a safe way.

♦ While we might deeply care about each other, we are not called to be caretakers who are responsible for solving anyone's problems or fulfilling anyone's desires.

6. Process Review

This is a time when the group can reflect on how it has done its work. Did we do what we said we wanted to do? Are there ways that we might do it better? Was everyone attended to appropriately? Were there moments when someone had the sense that the Spirit was at work in our midst? Were particular events in the session experienced as blocking or opening up the spiritual and relational potential? What gifts, issues, and patterns are emerging over time as we gain more experience with each other and the group as a whole? Are there modifications we can make to the group's patterns that would help the group better fulfill its purposes, or is there behavior from a member (or members) that needs to be lovingly confronted or addressed? These, and other considerations that will be discussed in chapter 7, are the kinds of ways the group can do its self-reflection. The housekeeping matters of who will do what and when and where also should be addressed here. Normally the process review period does not require much time in the session. But I recommend that a group build five to ten minutes into the regular flow of its meeting for this purpose. Ongoing monitoring and adjustments are easier on a group than having problems erupt because there has not been a regular time provided for addressing the needs and questions of the group and its members. The members might wish to schedule a longer process review after the group has been operating for a while, allowing for a deeper examination of its patterns and appreciation of the way it is meeting its goals, and providing for adjustments that are indicated.

7. Closing Ritual

As with the opening of the group, it is important to provide a good, clear closing. It need not be elaborate. As with the opening ritual, it might be as simple as carefully extinguishing a candle, ringing a bell or chime, or leading a prayer. Sometimes I will ask the members to offer a word or phrase or image into the "sacred bowl" of the group that summarizes their experience of the session. Ken Reid, my former clergy group facilitator, as a way of closing the session, encouraged members of the group to say what we were taking away from the meeting. A good closing of the group session provides the companion bookend to the group's opening. It values the sacred time and space that the group's members have shared enough to recognize the completion and fulfillment of that special time that we have dedicated to each other and to God.

We have looked at the core elements of group purpose, time, size, and structure, and noted that there will be many variations on these general guidelines due to particular group needs and contexts. In chapter 7 we will further discuss general small-group leadership issues and dynamics.

In the next four chapters, we are going to look in detail at ten models of spiritual companionship small groups. All of these groups share the core elements we have discussed as common characteristics, although the structure or other elements might be modified to accommodate the group's focus. I have divided these ten groups into four functional categories:

- Groups for Sharing Spiritual Practices and Exercises: *Circle of the Spirit, Holy Reading, Contemplative Prayer*

- Groups for Cultivating Inner Awareness and Discernment: *Spiritual Friends, Dreamwork, Communal Dreaming*

- Groups for Building a Spiritual Community of Support: *Benedictine Community, Companions in Transition*

- Groups for Compassion and Social Action: *Healing Prayer, Covenant for Justice and Peace.*

In addition to these ten models of spiritual companionship groups, we will look at an eleventh model for providing peer supervision and consultation for leaders of spiritual companionship groups. The *Leaders Group* model will be presented at the end of chapter 7.

chapter three

Groups for
Sharing Spiritual
Practices and Exercises

AMIDST THE MANY treasures of the Christian spiritual tradition are those practices that open up our capacity to pray and meditate and to encounter God's living presence through Scripture. The following three group models encourage awareness of the Holy One's immediate presence through the avenues of imagination, Holy Scripture, and silent prayer. All of these models are offered as templates to be used and modified as needed in order to best address the particular situation and interest of the spiritual companionship group.

Model 1:
Circle of the Spirit

> *Where can I go from your spirit?*
> *Or where can I flee from your presence?*
> *If I ascend to heaven, you are there;*
> *if I make my bed in Sheol, you are there.*
> *If I take the wings of the morning*
> *and settle at the farthest limits of the sea,*
> *even there your hand shall lead me,*
> *and your right hand shall hold me fast.*
> *—Psalm 139:7–10*

Focus

Members are led through spiritual exercises that are windows to the soul, using imagination and creativity as pathways to inner encounters with the Spirit of Christ/Wisdom or other interior expressions of God's presence.

Background

The use of the imagination in meditation and other creative ways to encounter the sacred is not a new spiritual practice. Scripture is filled with metaphorical language and stories that fire our imaginations and give us various images of God. One of the key aspects of the classic illuminative stage in the spiritual life is to so internalize the sacred Scripture stories about the biblical people of God and the life of Jesus that these stories can be drawn upon to illuminate our lives and guide us in the situations and events that challenge us.

In the sixteenth century, Ignatius of Loyola compiled some of the spiritual practices and exercises that had had an impact in his own formation into his *Spiritual Exercises* for the purpose of shaping retreatants, under the guidance of a director, in their own journeys into deeper life service to Christ. Many of the exercises are what we now call guided imagery meditations, where the retreatant imaginatively enters into a biblical or theologically-based scene and encounters the images as a lived experience evoking thoughts, feelings, desires, prayer, and greater awareness. There is an expectation that the exercises help the retreatant encounter God's love and desire for him or her and serve as a vocational guide. Many people have taken Ignatian retreats (or retreats that have been influenced by Ignatian spirituality), and many others have found their lives deepened because of the recognition of the role that our imagination and our feelings play in our spiritual life.

Group Form

Circle of the Spirit is a basic spirituality group. It is a model for spiritual directors or formation leaders who wish to familiarize their participants with a wide range of spiritual exercises. I developed this model as my final-year project for The Upper Room's Academy for Spiritual Formation (1988–90) and began using it in my parish when I served as a parish priest. Often I used this model during special seasons such as Advent, the season after the Epiphany, or Lent. One of these groups continued for five years in another setting and has had a lasting effect on its members. The structure of the group evolved into the basic structure for small groups for spiritual companionship discussed in chapter 2: opening ritual; check-in; leading the group in a spiritual exercise; providing a period for silent reflection and journaling; group sharing about the experience and its implications; process review; and closing ritual. It is particularly helpful in this group form to provide opportunity for some quiet personal reflection and then to invite participants to share what they wish about their experience with the exercise. Because this group is likely to use ninety minutes or more (depending on the group's size), it does not easily fit into a church's Sunday morning education hour slot.

Several potential outcomes are possible with the *Circle of the Spirit* group. First, a wide range of spiritual exercises and practices can be explored, so the longer a member participates in this group, the greater the repertory available to her or him for personal or shared use outside the group. Second, this group is likely to stretch the individual member's vision of how the Holy One can speak to us. Different exercises are going to affect people in different ways. An exercise may have profound impact on a particular person and have little influence on another group member, or even be experienced negatively. Exploring why this might be so in respectful group sharing of reflections can broaden our appreciation for how the Spirit engages people in different ways, discloses our resistances and sensitive spots, and broadens our appreciation to the fact that we are not all the same. Third, and most important, participation in this kind of group will hopefully school participants in how situations and events in ordinary times in life might be occasions for encounters with the Divine Mystery.

Carolyn Stahl Bohler's *Opening to God* was my introduction to guided imagery meditations based on Scripture. After using meditations from that collection for my own growth and understanding and then in groups on many occasions, I began creating my own guided meditations. Some of these meditations were based on Scripture, and others were designed for a meeting with the meditator's inner Wise One or some other figure. In the meeting with the inner Wise One the scenario runs something like this:

Meeting the Inner Wise One

1. Take a few deep breaths and invite God to be with you in your meditation and to provide guidance for the direction this imaged prayer will take.

2. If you feel comfortable doing so, close your eyes and imagine that you are standing in a green meadow with a forest bordering it.

3. Look around and notice what you see and feel. Notice how the ground feels beneath your feet. Notice the sky overhead and the sights and sounds you see and hear around you. Do you have a companion with you? Or are you by yourself?

4. Now imagine that there is a narrow dirt path near you that leads up a small hill. If you feel comfortable doing so, walk on that path, up the hill, to the place where the Wise One stays.

5. When you reach the door to the house of the Wise One, knock on the door and enter when you are bidden to do so.

6. Look around the room and look at the Wise One. What do you see in the room? Who or what does the Wise One look like to you?

7. You may have a question for the Wise One or you might wish to tell the Wise One about something that you are now considering. Ask the Wise One's counsel on whatever you wish, and listen for his or her reply. If you need further clarification, feel free to engage in further conversation with the Wise One.

8. The Wise One may say that she or he has something for you. It may be a special word or phrase, an object, a song, or some other gift. Receive the gift if the Wise One offers it, and feel free to ask about it if you need to know more. Respond to the Wise One's gift in whatever way you think is appropriate.

9. It is now time to say farewell to the Wise One. Do so, and then go to the door... walk down the hill on the path... and to the meadow... remembering your time with the Wise One and the gift you received, knowing also that you can visit your inner Wise One again. Whenever you are ready, open your eyes and bring your attention back to the group.

When I lead a guided imagery meditation, I explicitly give people freedom to do whatever they feel they should in their meditation and not do anything they feel they shouldn't. Safety and freedom are critical for the participants. I also acknowledge that at times some members will imagine things vividly and other times they may not. They should simply engage the meditation as best as they are able. Furthermore, if anyone is having difficulty with weak ego boundaries, where it is sometimes difficult to distinguish between reality and fantasy due to illness or medication or any other vulnerability, they may simply think about the scenario and not try to enter it with their imagination.

Leading people into soul work through imagination can be a powerful experience. One time I led a small group at my church in a guided imagery meditation based on Jesus' invitation: "Listen! I am standing at the door, knocking; if you hear my voice and open the door, I will come in to you and eat with you, and you with me" (Rev. 3:20). An elderly woman who had a heart of gold but was a bit brittle in her close relationships encountered in that meditation the all-embracing love of God in the image of Jesus' presence with her. When she reflected on how she experienced the meditation, overcome with emotion she said, "I just never knew that God could love me so much." It was a wonderful threshold moment for her, and whether or not it was the cause of subsequent changes, it certainly signaled a shift in the quality of loving that she would bring to her relationships. She had experienced a new depth in her knowledge of God's love for her, and she seemed to become freer to let her own love flow from that Source.

The *Circle of the Spirit* spirituality groups that I have led or coached have used a wide range of spiritual exercises and have not been restricted to guided imagery meditations. We have walked labyrinths, meditated on icons, held a "holy gaze" to each other (*darshan*), listened for the voice of God in nature, created our own mandala, chanted, practiced qigong and tai chi movements and other forms of moving meditation together, listened to the wisdom of our bodies, taken contemplative walks, drawn a "picture of my reality" or created a montage to that effect, worked with clay, and engaged in many other forms of spiritual exercises. Over a period of months, and sometimes years, the group members build up an acquaintance with a broad spectrum of spiritual exercises to draw upon for developing their own personal spiritual practice.

This group model also introduces members to other group forms of spiritual companionship. In *Circle of the Spirit* groups, I have sometimes led a series of sessions exploring a particular topic: group forms of *lectio divina* (holy reading), dreamwork in a small-group setting, group contemplative prayer, assisting each other in spiritual discernment situations, and engaging various practices related to an embodied spirituality. So, the *Circle of the Spirit* model introduces members to a variety of spiritual exercises for informing and supporting their personal practice. It is an excellent gateway into other forms of spiritual companionship, and stands on its own merit as an ongoing spiritual companionship group for support, spiritual formation, and mutual guidance.

Clearly, there is a lot of versatility in the kind of spiritual exercises that can be explored in a *Circle of the Spirit* group. I have provided an Appendix of some *Circle of the Spirit* exercises that might be used in a group. Many of these exercises could be used by groups in various religious traditions or in interfaith groups, and some could be used in secular settings.

Resources

Carolyn Stahl Bohler, *Opening to God: Guided Imagery Meditation on Scripture*. Sadly, this volume is often out of print, but I highly recommend its three chapters that provide an excellent introduction to using and leading guided imagery meditations.

Avery Brooke, *Learning and Teaching Christian Meditation.* A good basic read on Christian approaches to meditation that would be useful to leaders.

Anthony de Mello, S.J., *Sadhana, A Way to God: Christian Exercises in Eastern Form.* I use this as a required text in teaching the *Circle of the Spirit* group model. De Mello provides a wide variety of spiritual exercises (forty-seven in all), many of which can easily be adapted to group use, and gives us helpful comments about these exercises in a Christian contemplative context.

Tilden Edwards, *Living in the Presence: Spiritual Exercises to Open Our Lives to the Awareness of God.* This is another required text when I teach the *Circle of the Spirit* model. The volume is born out of the experience of leadership training at Shalem Institute of Spiritual Formation in Bethesda, Maryland, in small spiritual formation groups with a contemplative context. Edwards gives us particular exercises, topical discussion of some of the dynamics of these groups, and explores various dimensions of spiritual life.

Marlene Halpin, *Imagine That! Using Phantasy in Spiritual Direction.* One of the early books on guided imagery meditation with fifteen meditations by a Dominican sister.

Gerald G. May, *Pilgrimage Home: The Conduct of Contemplative Practice in Groups.* The late Gerald May described some of the early work on group formation at Shalem Institute. The book contains spiritual exercises as well as observations on small-group dynamics as they engage in contemplative practice.

Model 2:
Holy Reading

> *Indeed, the word of God is living and active, sharper than any two-edged sword, piercing until it divides soul from spirit, joints from marrow; it is able to judge the thoughts and intentions of the heart. And before him no creature is hidden, but all are naked and laid bare to the eyes of the one to whom we must render an account.*
> —*Hebrews 4:12–13*

Focus

The *Holy Reading* group provides support for members' personal and communal engagement with Scripture, often with a contemplative approach, that invites encounters with the Word of God amidst the words of the text.

Background

Besides the formational (rather than informational) emphasis that guided imagery meditation based on Scripture affords its practitioners, Scripture can be approached in other deeply formational ways that help to bring us into the presence of the Holy One, the living and active Word. Meditating on Scripture is an ancient practice. In the desert elders era of Christian experience (from about the fourth to sixth century), the practice of being given "a word" was common. People would go to an abba or amma and ask, "Give me a word that I may live." The spiritual guide would often give the seeker a verse or phrase from Scripture to meditate upon, sometimes for years. It was as if the word was planted in the heart and slowly grew in meaning and gave shape and direction to the seeker's life.

In the third century, Origen first used the term *lectio divina* (holy reading) to emphasize the importance of engaging Scripture with attention, constancy, and prayer. The term *lectio divina* was taken up by monastics in the fourth- to sixth-century rules for their communities to recognize the importance of regular reading and praying with Holy Scripture. However, there was no attempt to provide a *method* of prayerful engagement with Scripture until Guido the Carthusian in the twelfth century. This monk suggested four movements in the process of *lectio divina* that became the classic understanding: reading (*lectio*), meditation (*meditatio*), prayer (*oratio*), and contemplation (*contemplatio*). This personal engagement of Scripture through *lectio divina* has continued to the present time as a contemplative engagement through Scripture with the Holy One. Biblical scholar M. Robert Mulholland, Jr., has suggested adding silence (*silencio*) as the actual beginning of the process and incarnation (*incarnatio*) as the concluding movement. We begin the process with an open and expectant silence, a holy silence, and at the end have discovered that we are bearers of the Word. The Word has become incarnate within us and we bring it anew to the world.[1] We will go over the movements of *lectio divina* in greater detail a little later.

A communal form of engaging Holy Scripture contemplatively with some of the movements of the classic form of *lectio divina* has become popular. Variously called Group *Lectio Divina,* African Bible Study, and Oral Tradition Bible Study, it seems to have its genesis both in oral tradition methods in some of the African churches and in Latin American Christian community approaches to Scripture.

Group Form

Leaders of a *Holy Reading* small group can draw on a number of ways of engaging Scripture creatively and contemplatively. I am going to mention several methods in some detail as examples, but will also provide good resources to expand your options. The structure of the group's time will need to be modified depending on whether there is ongoing group reflection in the particular exercise or if it will call for this after some personal engagement with Scripture. The other movements—opening ritual, check-in, leading the exercise, process review, and closing ritual—will be a constant, regardless of the method you present to the group, if time allows. Many of these methods can also be presented in a church's educational hour, although the group would miss some of the core elements such as opening and closing rituals, process review, and check-in time.

One way to lead the group in engaging Scripture is by briefly introducing the classic movements of *lectio divina* (perhaps modifying this by adding holy silence/*silencio* at the beginning and ending with incarnation/*incarnatio* based on Robert Mulholland's suggestion). After the introduction, move into a brief silence, and read a Scripture passage aloud slowly and clearly (and perhaps give participants a printed copy of the passage). Next, allow quiet time of ten to fifteen minutes for everyone to practice a short period of *lectio divina,* then call everyone back to the group using a bell or chime, and invite reflection about what they discovered in their encounter with Scripture and the Word.

A Group Lectio Divina Process

1. The leader prepares the group for a period of *lectio divina.* The leader then invites the group to engage a passage from Scripture silently for a specified period of time, being open to anything that may arise that speaks to the group's situation. The members may discover themselves moving in and out of various stages in the process as noted below, rather like a dance with the Holy One. They are *not* expected to move through every stage. During the sustained silence, group members may be seated or quietly move about. They are free to draw, write, or remain still.

2 The leader then invites the group into a short time of receptive silence.

3. The passage is then read aloud slowly.

4. Silence is maintained for the allotted period of time.

5. The silence is ended. A simple "Amen," or a chime, bell, handclap, or repeating of the Scripture brings the group out of the silence.

6. The leader invites the group members to share whatever came from their prayerful engagement of Scripture that might help form the group and its community's direction.

Typical Movements in Lectio Divina

Silencio—preparatory silence.

1. *Lectio*—Reading
   Encountering Scripture in a way that allows the living Word to engage you, looking for the portion of text, phrase, or scene that has some energy for you and your community.

2. *Meditatio*—Meditation
   Thinking about the Scripture passage with energy for you, ruminating on the text or phrase or scene, wondering how this connects with or challenges you and your community.

3. *Oratio*—Prayer
   Gut-level prayer; dialogical, wrestling with personal and communal implications, willing to own your resistance or concerns as well as the desire to follow God's will, in touch with affective dimension.

4. *Contemplatio*—Contemplation
   Resolution and resting in the peace of God; a sense of having

discerned God's desire for you, or for some insight for your community, and a willingness to move in that direction.

Incarnatio—Incarnational effects
The Word has become flesh and dwells in you. How will you bring the fruit of your prayer into the world?

The following method is popular in spiritual direction circles and in churches. As previously mentioned, it goes by various names.

A Simple Group Form of Lectio Divina

A short passage of Scripture will be read three times during the course of the time together. Whoever is leading the process could provide background commentary on the Scripture passage before the first reading. Then the following steps are used, allowing ample reflective silence between the reading of Scripture and the peoples' responses:

1. Before the first reading, ask people to listen for the word, phrase, or image that catches their attention, and invite people to a short period of preparatory silence. Ask someone to read the passage slowly.

2. Invite each person simply to report the word, phrase, or image to the group. Note: anyone may choose *not* to make a statement at any time in this process.

3. Ask someone else to read the passage again (opposite sex of first reader if possible; may use a different translation).

4. Invite participants to take a minute to recall (and write down if they need to) the word or phrase or image that caught their attention.

5. Invite each person to simply report the word, phrase, or image to the group.

6. Invite participants to think/write about: "Where does this passage touch my life (our community) today?"

7. Invite each person to share what they have written with the group.

8. Ask someone else to read the passage out loud again.

9. Ask participants to think/write about: "From what I have heard and shared, what does God seem to be inviting me (or this community) to do or be in these coming days?"

10. Invite each person to share what they have written with the group.

11. Conclude with group reflections and/or prayer from the group members.

12. [If this is part of a large-group process, representatives of the small groups may bring their reflections touching on the community to the large group.][2]

Whatever method is selected for the group, the intention is to move the members from simply thinking about the Scripture and its possible interpretations into an active engagement with the God who is active within us and in our midst. Scripture is the medium to which members bring head and heart, the whole of themselves and their life situations, into the interpretation. Scripture begins to interpret *them*. As the group practices this way of interacting with Scripture they may begin to see that *lectio divina* is a way of approaching all of our situations in life— that the events of living are also a kind of sacred text, and that God's desires and challenges await them in their prayerful engagement of the situations.

One *Holy Reading* group member summarized her experience in this way:

> We have read biblical passages aloud, listening to the words in vary-ing translations. We have created a safe place in which to share the concerns and blessings of our lives with others who prayed on our behalf. We have listened for God's voice in prayerful silence, in the words of Scripture, and in conversation with one another. This group has formed us in the way that we pay attention to Scripture and in the way that we pay attention to each other.

Resources

Carolyn Stahl Bohler, *Opening to God: Guided Imagery Meditation on Scripture.*

Linda L. Grenz, ed., *In Dialogue with Scripture: An Episcopal Guide to Studying the Bible.* This guide (published in various editions) pro-vides a wide range of group methods of engaging Scripture. This was a required text when I taught students to lead Praying with Scripture groups at Seabury. However, the articles are of uneven quality.

M. Robert Mulholland, Jr., *Shaped by the Word: The Power of Scripture in Spiritual Formation.* Excellent background for groups where Scripture is primary.

John A. Sanford, *The Kingdom Within: The Inner Meaning of Jesus' Sayings*. This now classic book by an Episcopal priest-Jungian psychotherapist first opened me to the inner dimension of scriptural meaning.

Martin L. Smith, *The Word Is Very Near You: A Guide to Praying with Scripture*. Smith, an Episcopal priest, retreat leader, and former monastic, has provided an extended reflection on *lectio divina*.

Walter Wink, *Transforming Bible Study*. Wink blows open the creative possibilities of engaging Scripture for children and adults.

Model 3:
Contemplative Prayer

> *Indeed [God] is not far from each one of us.*
> *For "In him we live and move and have our being";*
> *as even some of your poets have said,*
> *"For we too are his offspring."*
> *—Acts 17:27–28*

Focus

The *Contemplative Prayer* group serves to support members in developing a contemplative approach to living through the shared practice of contemplative prayer and meditation and reflections emerging from that practice.

Background

In the 1960s the well-known Trappist monk Thomas Merton brought the notion of contemplative prayer out of the cloister and into the realm of ordinary people seeking a deepened relationship with God. Also during that era Abraham Maslow spoke of self-actualization and peak experience, and Eastern religious teachers proclaimed practices that offered direct spiritual experience and unity with Ultimate Reality. Many of us at that time were hungry for unmediated encounter with the Divine, having tired of an overemphasis on rationalism, dogma, and doctrines. Merton's writings pointed to a mystical tradition in Christianity that had been quietly present for centuries but lost to most Protestants and many Catholics. Seminaries had courses in ascetical theology, but the concept failed to reach into the churches, which tended to maintain contemplative prayer only as a higher prayer form that was the special vocation of certain monastics.

It would be outside the scope of this book to give a full background on contemplative prayer in its various forms. But a brief discussion is important. In the early Eastern church various simple repetitive prayers developed—called *hesychastic* prayer (from the Greek *hesychia*—silence, quietness, peace) or prayer of the heart. These prayers are said, sometimes with prayer beads or knotted rope, in rhythm with the breath. The *Trisagion* is one such prayer that sometimes shows up in our Western liturgies from ancient Christian sources:

> Holy God,
> Holy and Mighty,
> Holy Immortal One,
> Have mercy upon us.

Another of these repetitive prayers, the Jesus Prayer, rapidly spread in the West in the 1970s and beyond. The long version of the prayer is:

> Lord Jesus Christ, Son of God,
> have mercy on me, a sinner.

The Jesus Prayer can be shortened, even down to simply saying (in the heart) the sacred name *Jesus* to the rhythm of the breath.

In the Western church *The Cloud of Unknowing,* a fourteenth-century guidebook on contemplative prayer by an anonymous English monastic spiritual director, became widely read and used in the 1970s. That work, along with the practice of *lectio divina,* came together in the development of a contemporary version of contemplative prayer known as centering prayer. Popularized by Cistercian monks Thomas Keating and the late Basil Pennington, centering prayer has become a strong movement today. Similarly, the late Benedictine monk John Main saw the growth of Christian meditation centers in various countries.

There are some differences between these advocates of contemplative practice. Father Thomas Keating and his Contemplative Outreach, Ltd. organization emphasize the use of a centering word only when the one who is praying becomes aware that her or his mind is becoming distracted from a silent, open intention to let go of all for God. Here are the simple centering prayer guidelines from Contemplative Outreach:

Centering Prayer Guidelines

1. Choose a sacred word as the symbol of your intention to consent to God's presence and action within.

2. Sitting comfortably and with eyes closed, settle briefly and silently introduce the sacred word as the symbol of your consent to God's presence and action within.

3. When you become engaged with your thoughts, return ever so gently to the sacred word.

4. At the end of the prayer period, remain in silence with eyes closed for a couple of minutes.[3]

John Main advocated repetitious use of a centering word rather like a mantra or a prayer of the heart, showing the influence of Eastern forms of practice (he was first taught meditation in India by a guru, and then became a Benedictine monk). At the beginning of all of John Main's books, there is the following direction on how to practice contemplative meditation:

> Sit down. Sit still and upright. Close your eyes lightly. Sit relaxed but alert. Silently, interiorly begin to say a single word. We recommend the prayer-phrase "maranatha." Recite it as four syllables of equal length. Listen to it as you say it, gently but continuously. Do not think or imagine anything—spiritual or otherwise. If thoughts and images come, these are distractions at the time of meditation, so keep returning to simply saying the word. Meditate each morning and evening for between twenty and thirty minutes.[4]

My first group experience of contemplative prayer came twenty-five or so years ago, after conversation with my spiritual director of that time, the Reverend Fred Cunningham. We both read Gerald May's book *Pilgrimage Home*, which described Shalem Institute's experience of leading contemplative prayer groups. Their approach, which I have adopted, shied away from prescribing what everyone was supposed to do during the shared silent prayer time but encouraged using a focus word or object to help the group gently center down. Fred organized a group that met weekly during the season of Lent. After that initial commitment, some of us wished to continue meeting on a monthly basis, which we did for about a year.

The pattern we used for this contemplative prayer group was this: After some gentle body stretches, the leader brought us into the silence by simple chant, or brief Scripture reading, or bell. We then spent a period of about thirty minutes of silence together. After the formal period of silent prayer in a circle, we had about a ten-minute period we called the "silence after the silence." That was a time when members could quietly move around and, if they wished, make a journal entry and think about what they experienced in the silence or how this way of praying informs their life. Then we re-gathered for about a twenty-minute period of sharing our thoughts and experiences. Following that, the leader quietly closed the session.

A definition of the word *contemplative* was earlier offered as an endnote, and this is a good place to repeat Tilden Edwards's excellent description: "By *contemplative* I mean attention to our direct, loving, receptive, trusting presence for God. This attention includes the desire to be present through and beyond our images, thoughts, and feelings."[5] With this definition in mind, we can understand that on the "Spiritual Paths and the Landscape of Prayer" graph in chapter 1, those who wish to practice in a *Contemplative Prayer* group are likely to engage the heart and mystic dimensions. To call it contemplative prayer in a strict sense, the prayer is most likely to rest eventually in the affective and *apophatic* realm. I say *eventually*, because for most people their prayer will *begin* in the affective and *kataphatic* (heart path) dimension. Most people are actually engaging in meditation, and sometimes, like with *lectio divina*, the meditation might lead to contemplation. How does this play out in practice? Many participants will describe images and feelings that they experienced during their prayer (heart) that may bring them some sense of God's presence. Some will speak of their attempts to learn how to not get hooked on the various images that float past their consciousness. A few will describe the self-forgetful, emptied, imageless, intuitive openness of simply being present to the Mystery that is in-and-beyond all (mystic path).

Group Form
I was host of and participant in a small *Contemplative Prayer* group that met during the academic year for about twelve years. We took turns leading our fifty-minute sessions. We met in our sunroom where there were chairs and a couch with a glass coffee table and an oil lamp in the middle. The structure was simple.

Shared Silent Prayer Group

1. Light the lamp on coffee table as people start arriving.

2. Informal check-in as members gather for 10–15 minutes.

3. The session's leader offers a poem, prayer, chant, and/or chime or singing bowl.

4. Shared silence for 20–25 minutes.

5. Leader ends the silence with a chime, singing bowl, or other simple action.

6. Sharing whatever reflections members wish for about 10 minutes.

7. Quick process review, primarily to arrange a leader for next session.

8. Extinguish the lamp as people are leaving.

At the seminary I periodically offered and oversaw a *Contemplative Prayer* group for students to take as a course. The structure I used for that group is an adaptation of the one previously described and practiced that was derived from Gerald May's *Pilgrimage Home.*

Outline for a Contemplative Prayer Group

1. Opening the Group (1–2 minutes)
   Simple action such as lighting a candle, ringing a bell, or playing quiet music.

2. Check-in (2–3 minutes per person)
   Members invited to briefly share concerns, joys, and current events in their lives.

3. Shared Silence (20–30 minutes)
   Introduced with a brief reading, chant, bell, etc.

4. Silence After the Silence (10–15 minutes)
   Time for quiet movement, journaling, personal reflection on the experience of the shared silence.

5. Group Reflection (20–30 minutes)
   Group re-gathers and is given an opportunity to share what emerged from the silences and to make connections with a developing contemplative awareness in life.

6. Closing the Group (1–3 minutes)
   Leader closes the group with a simple action such as offering a brief closing prayer, or sharing the peace, or extinguishing a lighted candle.

When I teach this group method as a class for prospective group leaders, I add about twenty minutes to the session for a process review *after* the closing to give the session's leader feedback, for the group to explore the dynamics of the session and the group's life over time, and to reflect on assigned texts if that has not come up during the group reflection time. If this group is to be structured outside of training, I recommend a short ongoing process review period prior to closing the session.

It may be helpful for people to have something to do with their hands, eyes, or ears during extended periods of silence. Some find it helps them center down to hold a smooth stone, cross, rosary, or other object. Others might want to alternate sitting with slow meditative walking or tai chi or qigong movements. A simple visual focus such as a candle, icon, or mandala can also help members quiet themselves. I often like to use a singing bowl's sound to move people into and out of the silence. Chant can become an entranceway into the silence.

Similar to the notion that *lectio divina* can ultimately be a way of approaching all life events and situations as sacred texts, the leader can help the group engage this contemplative practice in such a way that it forms its participants in seeing the potential for contemplative awareness in all moments of living. There is nowhere God is not. All is sacred ground. Our actions and responses in life can be affected by the way we approach living always in the Presence. Often the contemplative literature speaks not so much on immediate effects of this way of praying or meditating (and frequently cautions against looking for short-term consolations) but on the formation that occurs over a long time. We may not recognize any big change in our prayer (or ourselves) over time, but others may see a transformation in us—the gentle work of the Spirit by the fruits produced in and through us.

Resources

Anonymous, *The Cloud of Unknowing*. A classic English fourteenth-century guide to contemplative prayer and the basis for centering prayer and Main's Christian meditation movements.

Anthony Bloom, *Beginning to Pray*. A simple, gentle work on contemporary Orthodox contemplative prayer in the Jesus Prayer tradition.

Cynthia Bourgeault, *Centering Prayer and Inner Awakening*. A good exposition on centering prayer and other kinds of contemplative practices, although an apologetic for the centering prayer method.

Brother Lawrence of the Resurrection, *The Practice of the Presence of God*. A classic seventeenth-century Carmelite treasure.

Thomas H. Green, S.J., *When the Well Runs Dry: Prayer Beyond the Beginnings*. One of the best introductions to contemporary contemplative prayer, drawing from sixteenth-century Carmelite mystics Teresa of Avila and John of the Cross. Green's thesis is that there comes a time when everyone serious about prayer will experience the well running dry and be brought to the threshold of contemplative prayer. Unfortunately, many do not know that there is a contemplative tradition that offers guidance when this happens.

Thomas Keating, *Open Mind, Open Heart: The Contemplative Dimension of the Gospel* and *Intimacy with God: An Introduction to Centering Prayer*. Two of Father Keating's many books on centering prayer. Father Keating presents the psychological aspects of centering prayer alongside his theological understanding.

John Main, *The Way of Unknowing: Expanding Spiritual Horizons Through Meditation.* One of several books that are collections of presentations and teachings by Main before his death in 1982.

Gerald G. May, *Pilgrimage Home: The Conduct of Contemplative Practice in Groups.* Contains spiritual exercises as well as observations on small-group dynamics as they engage in contemplative practice.

Gerald G. May, *Will and Spirit: A Contemplative Psychology.* A great study on the psychological aspects of unitive experiences and contemplative practice by a psychiatrist who became one of the leaders of the spiritual guidance program at Shalem Institute for Spiritual Formation.

Thomas Merton, *Contemplative Prayer.* A classic text on contemplative prayer from the Trappist monk who opened up an understanding of contemplative prayer to the general public.

M. Basil Pennington, *Centering Prayer: Renewing an Ancient Christian Prayer Form* and *Centered Living: The Way of Centering Prayer.* I have often used Pennington's *Centering Prayer* as a required text because of his historical presentation on contemplative prayer, his openness to the Spirit's work in contemporary practices of contemplative prayer, and his guidance on the particular method of centering prayer.

Richard Rohr, *Everything Belongs: The Gift of Contemplative Prayer.* Rohr has the big picture in mind, contemplative awareness in living.

chapter four

Groups for Cultivating Inner Awareness and Discernment

IN THIS CHAPTER we will look at small groups that help to cultivate and nurture our vast inner resources, the inner world that we carry within us throughout our lives. The desert mothers and fathers spent considerable time in their cells meditating on that inner world, discovering that the inner world is the arena where big and little demons and angels contend for our attention. Jesus, in his fasting sojourn in the wilderness, was tempted by the devil. Was that temptation an exterior experience? Doesn't it seem more reasonable, and more in line with our own struggles with what is true and what is illusion, what is right and what ultimately diminishes, that the experience was an inner awareness of temptation and discernment of his sense of purpose and vocation?

There is a story of Siddhartha Gautama fasting and meditating under the Bo Tree for an extended time, seeking release from the cycle of suffering. As Siddhartha was nearing enlightenment, The Tempter (Mara) came to him in the form of various gods. Following three temptations, one final time the Tempter came to visit him and suggested that Siddhartha simply slip into Nirvana and forget about trying to teach anyone about the way to enlightenment because, claimed the Tempter, no one would believe him. Siddhartha resisted this final temptation, became the Buddha, and began his teaching and spiritual leadership.

As the Buddha, five hundred years later Jesus, and then the desert fathers and mothers would encounter the spiritual world with its mixtures of temptations and truth—so too we have our spiritual challenges and blessings to discern. In chapter 1 we discussed the possibility that groups can offer us windows to personal and communal awareness and that groups can help in the work of spiritual discernment. The groups in this chapter are particularly focused on awareness and discernment.

Spiritual Friends is a group spiritual direction model. The principal way of engagement in this group is helping a member explore his or her deepest inner truths and values, and ultimately helping the member listen within a situation or condition for the presence and guidance of the Holy One. A *Dreamwork* group assists the individual members in exploring multiple levels of meaning that can be revealed in their dreams. Carefully attending to the dreamer's images, feelings, aspirations, and challenges can ultimately lead us all to questions of discernment and the promptings of the Spirit. We will also look at a specialized *Dreamwork* group, what I am calling a *Communal Dreaming* group. This group's associative and interpretive focus is on the shared social, communal dimension of experience. With this group the attention is on the *community's* (rather than the *individual's*) self-awareness and discernment of God's call revealed through dreams that are about or seem to belong to the community.

Model 4:
Spiritual Friends

> *Incline your ear, and come to me;*
> *listen, so that you may live.*
> —Isaiah 55:3a

Focus
Spiritual Friends is a spiritual direction/companionship group through which members support each others' spiritual lives and discern God's presence and call in the particular context of their lives.

Background
Many cultures and spiritual traditions over time have used a group setting as a way to assist someone in sorting out complex issues related to the way a person is to live and the choices he or she makes in life. An Anglican priest from Sudan told me that it is the usual practice in his culture for someone facing a decision or needing support and direction in a situation to seek the guidance of a group of wise elders from the community who listen and pray and offer counsel.[1] Similarly, a Korean ordained minister who was exploring spiritual direction resources in the

Chicago area shared with me that she would be most comfortable if the spiritual direction occurred in a small-group setting, the usual context in her home country. Western European-American Christians also have made use of the group to assist individuals in their spiritual guidance. Alongside the influence of monasticism over the past seventeen hundred years of Christian experience, I want to highlight the historical contributions that the Society of Friends (Quakers) from the seventeenth century and Methodists in the eighteenth century have made to group spiritual companionship.

The Quakers have a strong tradition of being anti-hierarchical and radically democratic. The source of authority rests in insights gained through silent meetings focused on an awareness and attention to the Inner Light. Twentieth-century Quaker mystic and theologian Thomas Kelly wrote powerfully about that Inner Light, which Quakers believe is within each one of us:

> Deep within us all there is an amazing inner sanctuary of the soul, a holy place, a Divine Center, a speaking Voice, to which we may continuously return. Eternity is at our hearts, pressing upon our time-torn lives, warming us with intimations of an astounding destiny, calling us home unto Itself. Yielding to these persuasions, gladly committing ourselves in body and soul, utterly and completely, to the Light Within, is the beginning of true life. It is a dynamic center, a creative Life that presses to birth within us. It is a Light Within which illumines the face of God and casts new shadows and new glories upon the faces of people. It is a seed stirring to life if we do not choke it. It is the Shekinah of the soul, the Presence in the midst. Here is the Slumbering Christ, stirring to be awakened, to become the soul we clothe in earthly form and action. And this Light is within us all.[2]

The Quakers developed the Clearness Committee to assist members in clearing out the clouds that hide the inner light of knowing what should be done in a situation calling for discernment. Clearness Committee meetings are marked by a prevailing environment of prayerful silence where members of the committee ask the kinds of questions that help the focus person sort through the issues and forces affecting a pending decision (should I take a particular job, make a move, marry this person, and so on). The clerk of the committee safeguards the process of the meeting(s) by assuring that there are no questions designed to elicit a particular response, providing for ample silence between questions, testing for consensus, and taking notes on the meeting for the member who is the subject of the gathering.

This form of group discernment has strongly influenced the Christian Vocations Project/Listening Hearts Ministries organization founded by Suzanne Farnham and others in the late 1980s. Their books on discernment, *Listening Hearts: Discerning Call in Community* and its companion volume *Grounded in God: Listening Hearts Discernment for Group Deliberations,* are excellent resources for individual and group deliberations on vocation and ministry. The method that Farnham and the Listening Hearts group uses for training teams to assist individuals in discerning vocational direction and life decisions is essentially a Clearness Committee process. Listening Hearts Ministries resources and its methods are increasingly used in Episcopal churches and other mainline Protestant churches.

Another contributor to communal spiritual companionship is the Methodist movement of the eighteenth century, with John Wesley's small-group system of spiritual nurture and guidance. The three groups were called classes, bands, and the select band. Danny E. Morris and Charles M. Olsen describe the class:

> The class was a small group of people who sought a personal relationship with God. The class leader was appointed by the Wesleys or their assistants and was a person with common sense, an experience of saving grace, and the ability to interpret the Bible to the members of the class. Each week the class leader would inquire about the spiritual state of class members, then offer prayer and guidance suited to the needs expressed by individuals.[3]

The next level of small group was the band:

> [The] focus of the band meeting was to deepen the participants' discipleship through obedience to the scriptural command to "confess your sins to one another, and pray for one another, so that you may be healed" (James 5:16). Members of the bands and the select bands were accountable to one another, and the will of God was discerned through dialogue, prayer, and experimentation.[4]

Finally, the select band (or select society) was a peer group, which included John and Charles Wesley:

> [The select band] provided guidance and support for people who had either the desire or the experience of perfect love: love of God with all one's heart, soul, strength, and mind.... The group's focus was on understanding and experiencing perfect love toward God and neighbor. Spiritual discernment was found in the interaction of group members.[5]

On the contemporary scene, The Upper Room's Academy for Spiritual Formation programs show the influence of this Methodist tradition in the development of their covenant groups as the primary small-group context for daily reflection and support by program members. When I participated in the two-year Academy from 1988 to 1990, we were all assigned to a small covenant group for the duration of the program. We took turns leading our covenant group, and when we led we had the option of meeting with a staff resource person to reflect on the group dynamics and receive support for any issues or needs for clarification on the process that might arise that week.

A further contemporary influence arises from the Shalem Institute's work in developing a form of group spiritual direction, described in the writings of Sister Rose Mary Dougherty. In that model the small group is composed of four to five people plus a facilitator, meeting for about two and a half hours once every four to five weeks. The participants take turns sharing about their ministry or something about their life, with times of silence and prayerful responses from the group to the presenter's situation. The facilitator watches over the group's process to assure a contemplative environment where the focus is more on the presenter than on the situation presented. The desire of the group is to assist the presenter in being in the immediate presence of the Holy Spirit and responsive to the guidance that God might provide.[6]

Group Form

The *Spiritual Friends* group combines some of the elements of Dougherty's group spiritual direction model with Listening Hearts. Further, it developed out of a *Circle of the Spirit* group that wished to give particular attention to each individual member as a group form of direction. So *Spiritual Friends* is a model that synthesized these other group forms. It can have more members in the group than Dougherty's Shalem model because not everyone is receiving the group's responses at each meeting. Like Listening Hearts, there is usually one focus person for the meeting, perhaps two if time allows and another member wishes to be the subject. Unlike Listening Hearts, the focus person does not need to be concerned about bringing a particular subject to the group for discernment—the presenter (focus person) is free to bring anything in his or her life to the group for the group's "sitting with," questions, prayer, and responses. As is the case with all the models, the primary focus is on the focus person and the group being in the immediate presence of the Holy One and being open and responsive to the guidance and love and support of God. Therefore the group should allow that spaciousness for silence and prayerfulness that helps ripen questions or thoughts or images and leads to greater relational depth.[7]

Guide to a Method of Group Spiritual Direction
in a Spiritual Friends Group

1. The facilitator signals the group's beginning.
   Call to begin, ring bell, Scripture verse, light candle, or other way to start.

2. Check-in period. This is a time of sharing what is going on in their lives, feelings, emerging situations.

3. The group makes a decision on who will be the (first) focus person. The focus person could be previously assigned or a spontaneous request emerging from the check-in.

4. The facilitator invites/guides the group into a state of silent deep listening and prayerfulness until the focus person is ready to present a situation or issue emerging from his or her life.

5. The group sits as spiritual friends with the focus person with her or his question/situation. This time is marked by unhurried, attentive, evocative questions that assist the focus person to explore her or his deep inner truth and sense of spiritual reality. This may continue until the focus person has a sense of being fully heard, held, and has attended to the Spirit *or* time necessitates concluding this period.

6. If time permits, some of the following could be explored:
   General discussion of what related issues emerged for others in the group.
   Attention to another group member's question/situation.

7. The facilitator attends to any assignments for next session or group concerns:
   Next facilitator? Focus person? Other group business? Process review?

8. The facilitator closes the group by inviting brief group prayer, leading a prayer, or ringing a bell.

The facilitator opens the group with a simple opening ritual and then leads the group into a check-in period. Next follows a group decision on who will be the focus person or persons. The group could establish a regular rotation of its members as the subjects of the group's focused attention. This arrangement has obvious advantages. It assures each member the opportunity to be held by the group for spiritual guidance and companionship. Further, it allows the focus person the chance to reflect upon and prepare in advance a presentation of his or her situation. However, the group should also consider having a process that allows a member spontaneously to request focused time at the session. Something may have come up recently that a member wishes to reflect upon with the group. Sometimes even in the check-in time it becomes apparent that a member might benefit from the group's attention. With this more spontaneous approach, it is important to assure that all members will receive sufficient focused attention over the span of the group's life.

I suggest that the group establishes a rotation of its members, with one person scheduled in advance to present at each session, while also allowing another member to request some group direction time if it is available. A group of six to eight members should be able to accommodate one or two focus people a session if it meets for one and a half to two hours. The facilitator might ask the group if anyone wishes unscheduled focus time at the beginning of the check-in period. With that knowledge, the leader and the group can allocate its time to better accommodate the needs in the session.

Following the check-in the leader turns the group's attention to the focus person. Calling for a period of sustained silent prayer is a pattern used both in Listening Hearts/Clearness Committee and in Shalem's group spiritual direction models—for good reason. The silence allows us to get past the "monkey mind" surface chatter that our Buddhist friends speak of and go deeper into a more receptive and intuitive place within and have a greater sensitivity for listening for the holy wisdom in the midst of the group.

The focus person is invited to present after a period of silence. After he or she makes an initial presentation, it is often helpful for the leader to ask if there are clarifying questions people would like to ask. Once the focus person has clarified the issue to everyone's satisfaction, the facilitator may invite the group into a period of silent prayer once again. After this second silence, the group helps the focus person explore his or her spiritual reality more deeply by asking evocative questions, offering images, and otherwise relating to the focus person as a spiritual director normally would to a directee. The facilitator tends to the focus person and group, seeing to an unhurried, prayerful pace that keeps the group open to the Spirit's guidance and away from opinionated or reactive or anxious conversation patterns.

The facilitator is also aware of time management of the whole session and is responsible for assessing what seems to be a sufficient period of exploration and sitting with the focus person. The facilitator checks with the focus person to see if he or she feels sufficiently companioned by the group. There may be concluding statements that the focus person and other members of the group wish to make. The facilitator may invite a short time of prayer (spoken or silent) for the focus person.

If there is a requested or assigned session with another focus person, the facilitator will invite a similar pattern of movements again. Or if there is time and desire from the members to discuss related issues or questions that emerged during the session, the facilitator can invite that conversation.

As the session nears its end, the facilitator should offer some time for reviewing the group's process and any housekeeping items, such as who will facilitate next time (if this role is rotated) and who will be a focus person. Some process assessment may have already happened in checking in with the focus person(s) about how they felt held and attended to. But group members may wish to address other dynamics in the meeting. Finally, the facilitator closes the group meeting with some simple ritual action.

Resources

Rose Mary Dougherty, *Group Spiritual Direction: Community for Discernment*. Description of a method of group spiritual direction developed by Shalem Institute for Spiritual Formation in Bethesda, Maryland. Contains excellent information on considerations of selecting members for a group and some of the dynamics of the group.

Rose Mary Dougherty, ed., with Monica Maxon and Lynne Smith, *The Lived Experience of Group Spiritual Direction*. A collection of descriptions of groups in various contexts. Useful in expanding the idea of group direction to other kinds of group formats and situations.

Suzanne G. Farnham, et al., *Listening Hearts: Discerning Call in Community* and *Grounded in God: Listening Hearts Discernment for Group Deliberations*. The Listening Hearts Ministries organization in Baltimore, Maryland, has produced two books as well as other materials. *Listening Hearts* provides helpful reflections on ministry and discernment. The model for group discernment in the appendix is based on the Quaker Clearness Committee. This book also contains an excellent annotated bibliography related to discernment. *Grounded in God* focuses more on principles for group discernment (rather than the group supporting individual discernment). Listening Hearts Ministries offers training and retreats.

Alice Fryling, *Seeking God Together: An Introduction to Group Spiritual Direction*. This work is a newer contribution to group spiritual direction literature. Fryling offers useful practical suggestions as well as provides a good background to the topic. Her suggested model in the appendix is similar to the *Spiritual Friends* model proposed in this book.

Model 5:
Dreamwork

I will bless God who teaches me,
who schools my heart even at night.
—Psalm 16:17 [8]

Focus

A *Dreamwork* group allows the members to explore the multiple dimensions of meaning in their dreams and can be a powerful way of listening for inner truth and wisdom. Working with dreams in this group setting will provide insights for both the dreamer and the group members, helping the dreamer find meaning in the dream.

Background

Texts about dreams are some of the oldest extant writings in human history. The Hebrew and Christian Scriptures contain many stories of dreams (sometimes referred to as "visions of the night") as sources of revelation of divine guidance or divine will for individuals, families, and nations. Sometimes the dreams had a sense of direct meaning, but at other times they required interpretation and discernment. The arguable prototype of the holy dream was when Jacob had stolen his brother Esau's birthright and was fleeing for his life:

> Jacob left Beer-sheba and went toward Haran. He came to a certain place and stayed there for the night, because the sun had set. Taking one of the stones of the place, he put it under his head and lay down in that place. And he dreamed that there was a ladder set up on the earth, the top of it reaching to heaven; and the angels of God were ascending and descending on it. And the LORD stood beside him and said, "I am the LORD, the God of Abraham your father and the God of Isaac; the land on which you lie I will give to you and to your offspring; and your offspring will be like the dust of the earth, and you shall spread abroad to the west and to the east and to the north and to the south; and all the families of the earth shall be blessed in you and in your offspring. Know that I am with you and will keep you wherever you go, and will bring you back to this land; for I will not leave you until I have done what I have promised you." Then Jacob woke from his sleep and said, "Surely the LORD is in this place—and I did not know it!" And he said, "How awesome is this place! This is none other than the gate of heaven." (Gen. 28:10–17)

For many ancient peoples and cultures, it was assumed that dreams were important messengers of divine wisdom and healing. It is beyond the scope of this book to explore the many powerful historical and multicultural approaches to dreams. Although the early Christians continued to look to dreams as a possible source of divine guidance but needing discernment, the prevailing attitude shifted slowly to skepticism or ambivalence as Aristotelian thinking gradually gained prominence. While some major religious leaders still held to the value of dreams (John Wesley, for example, in the eighteenth century), the rationalism and skepticism of the Enlightenment era marginalized dreamwork's value as a source of revelation and guidance.

Some artists and scientists continued to give credit to dreams as the sources of their creative work during the Enlightenment era, but the biggest reawakening to the power of dreams in the West came from psychoanalytic theory and its psychological applications in the early twentieth century through Sigmund Freud and in the depth psychology of Carl G. Jung. Episcopal priests John Sanford and Morton Kelsey, both profoundly influenced by Jung, became the first major mainline Christian proponents of the spiritual value of dreamwork in published books in 1968. There has been a gradual recovery in Christianity of the value of dreams, and that valuing has been apparent in the training of spiritual directors over the past thirty years.

Dreams *are* a gateway into imaged spiritual reality (Jacob's gate of heaven), into the soul, into many realms of living as individuals, families, societies, people sharing earth with other life, and in reflecting on our part in the vastness of the cosmos. Dreams are, among other things, a series of symbols. Symbols are multivalent; they have many levels of possible meaning and may mean a multitude of things to both the dreamer and to those working with the dreamer.[9] The symbols generate associations to past, present, and imagined future experience for the dreamer and her or his companions. Frankly, I find dreamwork to be a fascinating creative process. So a typical *Dreamwork* group will approach interpreting dreams with an eye to many different possible meanings—with respect for the dreamer as the one who determines what the dream ultimately means to him or her. However, in the process of dreamwork in a group the dream symbols will create many meanings for the other members as well as the dreamer—and some meanings might be shared by several or all members because they touch on a communal-social concern.

Listed here are some possible dimensions of meaning in dreams, ranging from the personal to the collective, that are helpful to keep in mind when working with a dream:

- Physical Health—watch for symbols of and/or commentary on the health and well-being of the body.

- Humor—look for the dream puns, Freudian slips.

- Personal Relationships—aspects that explore emotional energy in past and present relationships, sexual/libidinal desire (Freud).

- "Will to Power and Competence"—explores hopes, plans, projects, goals, issues of dominance/submission, in work and other areas of life interests (Adler).

- Personal Integrative—various images, persons in dream are parts of the whole self (Gestalt).

- Creativity—source of solutions to personal or collective problems, source of works of art.

- Archetypal Symbols—explores deep instinctual dimension of shared human drama within the "collective unconscious" (Jung). These universal symbols (Shadow, Wisdom Figure, Animus/Anima, Healer, etc.) appear cross-culturally, but are clothed by cultural contexts and particular circumstances.

- Societal—symbols of our shared social experience in organizations, society, nation, culture, global community; common concerns and challenges, hopes, fears, goals, frustrations, aspirations.

- Spiritual Development—numinous encounters with the holy (and evil) on personal or collective dimensions; source of inspiration, repentance, revelation, discernment.

Although we might get a clear, direct communication from Wisdom/God in a dream, it is reasonable to approach dreams with humility and operate under the assumption that most of our communications are filtered through our personalities, particular circumstances, religious beliefs and ideas of God, and culture. So our communications call for some degree of discernment and critical ability. Kelly Bulkeley offers some helpful thoughts about interpreting dreams for religious or spiritual meaning. He suggests we read the dream text or narrative with a hermeneutical eye, approaching that text like we would Scripture that is interpreted. So he offers these guiding principles for interpreting a dream:

1. We encounter a dream as a special kind of text, as something both strange and yet related to us.
2. We have a preliminary awareness of our subjective biases.
3. We are open to the dream and admit to not knowing what exactly will come of the interpretation.

4. We play with the dream, surrendering to a back-and-forth dialogue with it.

5. The criteria for a valid interpretation are how well it harmonizes the parts of the dream with the whole, how well it coheres with the rest of our knowledge, and how well it works out according to our practical needs and interests.

6. The ultimate goal of dream interpretation is to broaden horizons, open up new questions, and widen awareness.[10]

And then he adds these questions to help further illuminate possible religious dimensions:

1. What are the most prominent images in the dream?

2. Do the images metaphorically express religious or existential concerns?

3. What is the emotional power of the dream?

4. Does the dream relate to a current life crisis or transition?

5. Does the dream relate to both the dreamer's past and the dreamer's future?

6. What potentials does the dream have to transform the dreamer's waking life?[11]

In my work with spiritual discernment questions and the power of symbols to guide individuals and communities, I offer the following questions to help guide our understanding and discernment from a Christian perspective of the spiritual significance of the symbols that emerge in dreams and meditations and from other sources of revelation:

1. What is the source of this symbol that has emerged and holds power for us?

2. Is it life-giving even while it might be challenging?

3. Does it bring us beyond ourselves alone?

4. Does it speak to our deepest sense of truth?

5. Does it seem consistent with our best understanding of God's great desires for humanity as revealed in sacred Scripture and in the wisdom of our spiritual teachings?

6. Does it speak of the Paschal mystery, the way of the cross, and new life in Christ?[12]

It can be helpful for group or retreat leaders to keep these principles and questions in mind when engaging the power of symbols to evoke guidance. We can be discerning about them, for just because something may present itself as from God does not mean we should uncritically accept it as unfiltered and unmixed with other messages and forces (such as our own ego-driven projected desires masking as God's demands). And yet, we can also have the humility and willingness to say, with young Samuel in the nighttime: "Speak, for your servant is listening" (1 Sam. 3:10).

Group Form

I use a slightly adapted model of a *Dreamwork* group presented by Jeremy Taylor in his book *Where People Fly and Water Runs Uphill.* One of the safeguards he emphasizes is that group members use such language as, "If this were my dream ... " to qualify the possible interpretation or association offered to the dreamer.[13] This phrase makes it clear that a particular meaning or interpretation is not being imposed on the dreamer—who is free to accept that interpretation or not—but simply that the dream does have that meaning to the group member. This kind of offering of possible interpretations frees the dreamer and the group members to look for their own "aha!" of recognition of meaning but does not impose any meaning on anyone. The group's primary task is to assist the dreamer in exploring possible meanings, but it also wonderfully allows for meaning to emerge for other members and on a shared level.

Here's the model I most often use for *Dreamwork* groups:

A Dreamwork Group Design
for Spiritual Companionship

1. Brief Opening Ritual
   Open with some simple action that initiates the group's sacred time. It might be a song, lighting a candle, ringing a bell, a brief reading, or leading the group in a short prayer. Whatever the action, it is intended to mark the beginning of a time for group support, dream sharing, and honoring the divine gift and call to wholeness (shalom), which respects the physical, spiritual, emotional, intellectual, and communal dimensions of our lives.

2. Check-in Time
   Group members are invited to share what has been happening in their lives recently, how they are feeling, and anything else that they would like the group to know for their mutual support and building their group relationships.

3. Initial Dream Sharing
   All group members are now invited to share a dream. These dreams are received by the group without interpretation or much comment.

4. Preparatory Centering

The leader provides some entrance into a time of silence. Again, it might be by simply inviting the group to a specified period of silence. A chant, bell, brief prayer, or a short reading might initiate the silence. The purpose of the silence is to assist people in accessing a more receptive, intuitive, imaginative, contemplative mode of consciousness.

5. Focused Attention on a Dream

The focus person (dreamer) presents his or her dream in its entirety in the present tense. Group members may then ask questions for clarification. Then members may explore with the focus person various possible dimensions of meaning present in the dream—both to the focus person and to the other group members. Group members should avoid statements that interpret meaning for the focus person; rather, they should acknowledge their own projections of meaning for themselves. For example, use phrases such as "What this says to me is..." or "If it were my dream..." or "Are there things that you associate with...?" rather than "This means...."

The group may continue to work with the dream as long as it seems productive, or until it is time to move to closure. Jeremy Taylor has developed four questions that help determine when to close off dreamwork:

> – Has my own understanding of the dream been illuminated and deepened by the discussion?
> – Have most of the people in the group also had aha's (breakthroughs of meaning) while exploring the dream?
> – Has the dreamer experienced any aha's in the course of the work? (Note that more introverted members are less likely to experience aha's on the spot.)
> –Is it simply "clock time" to move on?[14]

The leader consults with the focus person and the group to see if it is time to move to closure (or begin work with another focus person and dream).

6. Final Reflections, Process Review, and Closure

The leader invites group members to reflect on all that has occurred in the dream session.

> Do any members need additional support or responses?
> Have new, shared levels of meaning emerged in the course of this time together?

Is there some new discernment or movement toward healing, justice, and shalom?

The leader then invites the group into a closing prayer circle, or the sharing of summary words or phrases, or some other simple ending to the sacred time.

This kind of group is lively and creative once people have determined that it is a safe and trustworthy place. The group leader needs to enter into this with confidence and the ability to coach members to explore different levels of meaning. Leading by example is helpful at the beginning, but avoid dominating by becoming the "expert." The dreamer is the real expert in discovering what is meaningful. But we are all beginners when we explore the inexhaustible possibilities of symbols. Some members may say they do not remember their dreams, but even a little fragment can be mined for riches. One group member who "never dreams" offered that he could only remember a vague image of a plant on a hill. In being present with him and encouraging him to explore his associations with the image, the group helped him be in touch with how much he was missing gardening—and his readiness for new growth beyond seminary. That touched many other members since all were in a transitional place in their lives.

Resources

Kelly Bulkeley, Ph.D., *Transforming Dreams* and *The Wilderness of Dreams*. Bulkeley is active in the academic study of dreamwork and religion. His research is described at http://kellybulkeley.com/.

Dream Network Journal. This publication also maintains a website at http://dreamnetwork.net.

Patricia Garfield, Ph.D., *Creative Dreaming: Plan and Control Your Dreams to Develop Creativity, Overcome Fears, Solve Problems, and Create a Better Self*. This introduction to dreamwork originally came out in 1976 and has been regularly reprinted due to its popular writing style and appeal.

Carl G. Jung, *Memories, Dreams, Reflections*. This personal memoir of the noted depth psychoanalyst is well worth reading for an inside view of his theories and life.

Morton Kelsey, *God, Dreams, and Revelation: A Christian Interpretation of Dreams* and *The Other Side of Silence*. *God, Dreams, and Revelation*, an expanded study of dreams in Jewish and Christian history up to the modern era, is Kelsey's definitive approach to dreamwork. Along with John Sanford, Episcopal priest and scholar Morton

Kelsey broke new ground in the value of working with dreams in mainline Christianity. Kelsey's other books argue for experiential encounters with God. *The Other Side of Silence* is an extended study on kataphatic Christian spirituality and includes his thoughts on Christian meditation and dreamwork.

John A. Sanford, *Dreams: God's Forgotten Language* stands alongside Kelsey's writing as a major contribution to a Christian engagement with dreams. Sanford was an Episcopal priest and Jungian depth psychoanalyst, and his work speaks to the power of the archetypal level of dreams, both in Scripture and in current dreams.

Jeremy Taylor, *Where People Fly and Water Runs Uphill*. Taylor is popular in contemporary spiritual guidance circles due to this book and other writing and presentations. His description of a group method of dreamwork is the standard approach that I have slightly modified for my own use.

Model 6:
Communal Dreaming

> *Then afterward I will pour out my spirit on all flesh;*
> *your sons and your daughters shall prophesy,*
> *your old men shall dream dreams,*
> *and your young men shall see visions.*
> *Even on the male and female slaves,*
> *in those days, I will pour out my spirit.*
> *—Joel 2:28–29*

Focus
Communal Dreaming is a group form that explores the depth communal dynamics of life and the guidance of the Divine in and to a community or organization through dream-sharing. This approach to dreamwork is focused on the shared social levels of meaning.

Background
We have already mentioned that dreams and their symbols may be interpreted on many levels, with possible meanings ranging from the intra-personal to the global. Various cultures have held that dreams may have revelatory significance on the socially shared levels. Decision-making processes for the good of the tribal village in traditional Iroquois governance, Aboriginal Dreamtime consultations for decisions, the dream revelations of the Hebrew Scriptures' prophets, and early

Christian writers' views that some dreams are divinely sent provide historical evidence for considering dreams as a source for social guidance. Consider also the record of well-documented situations where dreams have been the source for scientific breakthroughs and material for creative products in the arts and literature, and a strong case can be made that important social benefits are derived from working with dreams.

Communities and groups can share their dreams, looking to the social levels of meaning that the dreams' symbols offer as guidance and insight for the collective soul. Some communities and organizations use dreamwork on a communal level as an aid to their discernment work—exploring the hopes, fears, aims, desires, frustrations, joys, structures, and much more that dreams can disclose about the community. Several members of the Sisters of St. Joseph in the Nazareth, Michigan, community were part of a Dream Team that met regularly for breakfast and shared their dreams for the wisdom they might provide this community. They helped organize a discernment process for the community focused in dream wisdom. One of the creative fruits of that work was the birth of the Transformations Spirituality Center.[15] In a different engagement of social dream facilitation, Pat Coughlin, O.S.B., worked with two religious communities in Chicago as the basis for her Doctor of Ministry thesis using the social dreaming matrix model developed by W. Gordon Lawrence.

Group Form
Sister Pat Coughlin's experience with those communities and my own study of Lawrence's writing helped form my own modification of the social dreaming matrix method for seminary small-group courses I facilitated—twice as the sole model and twice in combination with the *Dreamwork* group model. In the "Dream Matrix" course, students took the course time in their own social dreaming matrix session and reflected on what was revealed. At the conclusion of the course they offered a presentation to all interested people in the larger seminary community. They presented background material on social traditions of dreamwork and its communal benefits, reported some of their findings from their dream matrix sessions, and facilitated a brief dream matrix session that was open to visitor participation.

In the June 3, 2003, presentation to the Seabury community, I compiled the following notes on these learnings reported by the class:

◆ Dream matrix sessions can change the way that interactions occur within a community. Once a group begins to interact in a different way in a matrix, the community might see changes in other interactions.

- Because the matrix has transformational aspects, it provides a way toward transformation in the larger community.

- It changes the way we perceive things, and our worldview is changed. Working with our collective unconscious loosens things up a bit and we see things we couldn't see with our five senses.

- The group transforms the dream into a community connection—we look beyond ourselves—and become open to what the dream is saying for the community.

- It is a safe method to share information and explore.

Other comments from students about what they discovered included:

- It has awakened our understanding of the community and has made us aware of issues within the community.

- As a new person it is very revelatory to see what happens when the person offers up a dream to the community.

- We can never look at SWTS (Seabury-Western Theological Seminary) the same again.

- We learned how to surrender ourselves to the process—we haven't gotten any answers but we've asked lots of questions and named lots of themes.

- There is great support from the others in the matrix.

- Perhaps it moves us toward virtues? For the betterment of the community and for others?

- Learned the value of patience, being open, waiting.

Students also offered reasons for why this might be useful in other communities:

- Provides an avenue to freely explore meaning.

- It can reveal things about the community—the matrix group itself, the parish, the community that the parish is in, and the larger church.

- It needs safeguards, especially for those with some mental health issues where they cannot distinguish between normal reality and dream [or I would add, for those who are in particularly fragile emotional or physical states].

◆ It is helpful for those communities that want to continue
exploring [the spiritual and soul dimensions of their life
together].

Some dreams just seem to belong to a community. As an example,
here is one dream that emerged in a social dreaming matrix session at
Seabury-Western Theological Seminary, a dream we called "Seabury
Geckos and Dinos":

Scientists are running tests on animals at Seabury-Western Theological Seminary. There were some animals who seemed to have free
run around the lab—these were human-sized geckos. In the center
was a dome-shaped holding pen made out of glass and concrete.
Dinosaurs were inside and really wanted out. One was looking
around trying to figure out how to do that. The geckos surrounded
the pen and watched. When I told the scientist that the dinosaurs
were going to try to get out, she was unconcerned because "they
were too stupid."

In the "Dream Matrix" group's reflection time, we discussed how
this dream humorously touched on our anxieties about living in an age
where science is foremost and religion, at least mainline religion, is in
decline with antiquated structures. We wondered what needs to evolve
or die out in our seminary and in the education process there and in
the church at large. A few years later, while I was chaplain at the seminary, that dream came back to haunt me. Seabury was then on the
brink of financial collapse. No longer could it continue to exist in the
same way it had for the past one hundred fifty years as a residential
seminary based, said Gary Hall who was then dean and president, "on
a nineteenth-century model in the twenty-first century." In fact, the seminary made radical changes, releasing many faculty and staff and elim-
inating their residential program, and is trying to provide an alternative
model for the twenty-first century. Much of what had been the seminary's life has died. Some of its life is evolving into a new institution.

The following is the model of communal dreaming, an adaptation
of the Social Dreaming Matrix that I have introduced in seminary classes
and in other leadership formation programs:

Social Dreaming Matrix
for Communal Dreaming Groups

1. Simple Opening Ritual

2. Group Check-in

3. Prepare for Social Dreaming Matrix

4. Dream Matrix Session:
     Dreams are offered to the matrix
     Responses to the dreams focus on the *communal* dimension
     [Note that an *association* can include feelings, images, events,
          stories, etc.]
     Association to the matrix session or group itself
     Association to the particular community or organization
     Association to larger groups of which this community is a part
     Association to the broader church or world
     Association to other dreams

5. Break

6. Group Reflection and Process Review

7. Closing Ritual

Movements 1 and 2 are part of the usual spiritual companionship group process. In movement 3 two things happen. First, the facilitator instructs the group members to move physically out of the circle format that is common (where we look *within* the circle to see everyone) and places members in a different pattern that deemphasizes viewing others. The physical pattern might look like a circle with everyone facing *out and away* from other members. Another pattern we often used is to line up people, or circle up, like a train where we see the back of others' heads. Or we would form several small tight circles where people are facing outward. Gordon Lawrence likes to organize people into small beehive structures. The point is to structure things to give emphasis to listening to the voices that offer the dreams or associations as belonging to the whole group—the collective soul—rather than giving attention to who is speaking. After the group is physically resettled, a time for quieting people down is helpful before the facilitator (*Taker* in Lawrence's language) begins the social dreaming matrix part of the session. I like to use a singing bowl or chime to move people quietly into the matrix session.

The leader in movement 4 takes notes for the group during the matrix dreaming period, which might last anywhere from thirty to forty-five minutes if the whole session is ninety minutes. This period seems almost dreamlike to me. A dream is spoken by someone. Associations to the dream start emerging from the group like popcorn popping. There may be two or three dreams offered at any time in this period, with various associations to each of them emerging and playing off each other. The dreams do not need to relate directly to the community. However, the dreamer should have some feeling that the dream somehow belongs to the group/community. If someone starts to explore personal individual associations of meaning apart from the community, the leader should remind the group that what is being explored ought to relate to the shared life in this group or community or organization.

This is not a time for the group to give an analysis of what themes and patterns are coming up or do other secondary reflection on meaning. That will come later. This is a time for the group to give voice to its collective soul—to allow the group collective unconscious to surface. When the period of the social dreaming is over, the leader can note its end by the sound of a bell or chime or some other signal.

The group may want a brief break (movement 5), and rearrange the seating. People are now going to move into a time of reflecting on what emerged in the matrix. If a board is used for writing notes, then arrange the seating and board placement accordingly.

The leader then invites (movement 6) the group members to reflect on what themes or patterns or insights came up in the matrix period. What can we learn from the session about our life in this community? What has been disclosed about the soul of this community? If there have been previous sessions, are there patterns that point to something we need to be aware of that is part of life in this community or organization? If this is a tool of spiritual discernment, what guidance or wisdom or new awareness might God want us to know about the group or community? Are we being invited to be within the community in some way, or do something as a result of this session? After reflecting in this manner, the group session concludes with any process review observations and then a closing ritual (movement 7).

I would add that in the seminary matrix groups, whoever offered a dream in the session also e-mailed it to the other group members after the session. This provided additional opportunity for members to reflect on the dream or to offer insights on how the dream might be speaking about the community.

This is a fascinating process that can challenge those of us with a Western orientation to think more radically in communal terms—the community or group as a living organism—than our individualistic conditioning normally permits. In this view of dreamwork, the group has its own dreams—or dreams are seeking the group so that they can express their deeper, fuller meaning. Our consciousness and appreciation of a community can be greatly expanded by this process.

Resources

Pat C. Brockman, O.S.U., Ph.D., *The Community Dream: Awakening the Christian Tribal Consciousness*. A narrative of several communities' dreamwork experiences and the changes that occurred.

W. Gordon Lawrence puts forward his social dreaming matrix process through *Introduction to Social Dreaming: Transforming Thinking* and the other books he has written and edited with contributions from other consultants. This process is used with a variety of organizations, including churches.

chapter five

Groups for Building
a Spiritual Community
of Support

ALL THE SPIRITUAL companionship groups are supportive of group members, but the models presented in this section give particular emphasis to providing a community of spiritual and emotional support to the members as they live into the particular circumstances, challenges, and opportunities that are present in their lives.

Model 7:
Benedictine Community

> *That God may be glorified in all things.*
> *—1 Peter 4:11b*

Focus
This group works to build a covenant community founded on Benedictine spiritual principles that can be applied in their lives. This is a community of support for people who are interested in shaping their lives according to one of the great spiritual traditions.

Background
The *Benedictine Community* group draws on the rich fifteen-hundred-year tradition of Western Christian monastic experience as the basis for applying its spiritual principles to those who are living in the world

rather than in a cloistered religious community. The Benedictine tradition is the one by which I have been most deeply formed, and is relatively familiar to many Christians today. However, a group could be formed around Celtic, Franciscan, Ignatian, Carmelite, or other major spiritual traditions that are expressions of various Christian religious traditions.

Benedict (480–543) was born in the region of Nursia near Rome. What we know of St. Benedict comes from Gregory the Great's second book of the *Dialogues,* written some fifty years after Benedict's death. After becoming disillusioned with life in Rome, Benedict became a solitary in the region of Subiaco. While there, a neighboring monastery asked him to become their leader, but the differences between the community and his own practices caused such a conflict that the monks attempted to poison him. He returned to solitary living again for a short time. About 530 he went to Monte Cassino and undertook a preaching and prayer ministry and began forming monasteries. Benedict's sister, Scholastica, lived nearby and led a women's monastic community. Benedict edited and added to the various monastic rules existing in his time (especially the *Rule of the Master* and Augustine's counsel to religious communities) to create the *Rule* by which his monasteries are shaped. He is seen as the father of Western monasticism, and his *Rule,* adapted to particular circumstances, continues to be followed by over fourteen hundred communities in our time.

My own spiritual formation has been largely Benedictine. Since the late 1970s I have made retreats at St. Gregory's Abbey in Three Rivers, Michigan. As a parish priest in Michigan our parish's men's group looked forward to an annual retreat at this men's Episcopal Benedictine monastic community. I became an oblate of that monastery, taking life vows to support that community and to represent Benedictine spirituality in the world.

There are several ways that the spirit of Benedictine community has influenced my own household. For over twenty years my wife and I have shared a time of prayer together in the morning unless we are going together to worship with a larger community. Our time of morning devotionals has been adapted from the *Book of Common Prayer's* Morning Prayer service. Houseguests are always welcome to join us in this morning practice. We take turns leading the simple ritual: Light an oil lamp, chant or sing a hymn, read a psalm by alternating verses between each other, read a passage of Scripture from the daily office lectionary, meditate silently and perhaps comment on the Scripture, offer prayers from cycles of prayers and our intercession list and our own needs and concerns, add a concluding prayer, and close with singing the Lord's Prayer. When we have had young children in the home, we all gathered for an evening prayer time at the close of the children's day. Again we used a simple ritual that included simple chant and a Scripture story. In addition to lighting the lamp and extinguishing it at the close of prayer, the children loved to use our Irish bodhran drum, tincsha temple bells, and a rain stick throughout the prayer time. As children got older we would use the *Book of Common Prayer's* service of Compline to complete the day.

When our son was growing up, we started instituting weekly family meetings. Benedict, in chapter 3 of the *Rule,* makes it clear that the counsel of all the community, including the youngest members, is respected and valuable when deliberating on issues that affect everyone. Family meetings are a way of making sure that everyone in the family has the chance to bring their concerns and interests to be heard with respect. Everyone contributes to the meeting's agenda and takes turns leading the meeting.

The other thing we initiated with our son was a family covenant— a sort of community rule or framework of regular practices that helps the community live and grow in healthy ways. In the family covenant we acknowledged that we are mutually accountable for the family's well-being. We framed the covenant in terms of practices for physical care (including care of the house and financial stewardship); spiritual care (including daily, weekly, and special seasonal practices); care of the mind and family decisions (valuing education, family meetings); and emotional health (including recreational practices and resources to help us in tough times).

When I formed Benedictine Community groups at the seminary, I negotiated some elements in the structure with the group members. Always there would be a period for reflecting on the *Rule of St. Benedict,* using commentary by Sister Joan Chittister, O.S.B., or oblates Esther de Waal or Norvene Vest. I particularly like Chittister's *The Rule of Benedict: Insight for the Ages* because it divides the *Rule* into short daily readings with commentary that can be read through three times in a year. In addition there are a whole host of books on Benedictine spirituality that we could draw from for discussion and application. People often were interested in developing either a personal spiritual rule of life or a family (or community) covenant shared with those in their household. And we engaged in some form of community prayer and/or a spiritual practice such as *lectio divina.*

Here is an example of this model's structure:

Benedictine Community Group Process

1. Opening Prayer—A Collect for St. Benedict

   We pray you, Lord, to stir up in your Church the Spirit whom
   our blessed father Benedict, the abbot, served. Filled with the
   same Spirit, may we strive to love what he loved and do the
   works which he taught. We ask this through Jesus Christ your
   Son, who lives and reigns with you and the Holy Spirit, God,
   now and for ever. *Amen.*[1]

2. Check-in

   [brief break]

3. Community Reflections from such sources as:
      Assigned readings from the *Rule of St. Benedict*
      Sharing on spiritual exercises or practices
      Forming a rule/covenant

4. Process Review

5. Closing Prayer
      Morning/Noonday/Evening Prayer or Compline

I have also used this model for weekly sessions during Lent for a
parish study, begun with the requisite soup supper. There are other
churches that have a Benedictine Cell or small community that regularly
meets and follows a similar pattern. With the increasing interest in
Benedictine spirituality for those in mainline churches, I expect that
this form of group could be very popular. It also can be the basis for
more comprehensive intentional communities. I have had the privilege
of being a spiritual companion to several such intentional communities
where young men and women, some married and some single, have
decided to form a contemplative Christian community, share a household together, and live with a simple spiritual rule or covenant.

A rule of life is something that is associated with the intentionality
of Benedictine living. In Latin the word for rule is *regula,* and for a
community it is a guide for regulating its activities—setting up expectations around its regular practices. I like Joan Chittister's analogy of a
rule to a trellis—a framework or structure that allows something to
grow upon it. I see a rule of life as wholistic—a foundation for a person's or community's ongoing development that honors physical needs,
supports stable and respectful relationships, provides opportunities for
intellectual growth and creativity, and nurtures spiritual well-being that
attends and gives worship to the divine Source—and it is flexible

enough to adapt to changes in circumstances in life. Monastic vows to obedience, stability, and ongoing conversion for the well-being of the community intend to support a dynamic life rooted in Christ and related to people who together become a "school for God's service."[2] However, I want to emphasize that Benedictine spirituality is just one example of a major tradition that could become the basis for a small spiritual companionship community of support. A spiritual companionship community based on Franciscan spirituality would surely be attractive to some people and churches.

Bridging this model with the next are various kinds of covenant groups. Covenant groups (where there are promises of support and spiritual exploration together) for women's or men's spirituality, to name just two examples, could use this kind of group structure. I mentioned earlier that a men's group in the parish where I served as their priest used to look forward to a yearly retreat at a men's Benedictine monastery (sometimes at St. Gregory's Abbey and sometimes at a Lutheran priory called St. Augustine's House). The men's group formed themselves as the Brotherhood of St. John (named for the parish's patron saint). They were a men's spirituality and support group, where time was spent both in some form of Scripture study and in personal case presentations. Although they occasionally sponsored some service to the church, they did not want to be too task-oriented. What they wanted was a safe place to share with some depth about their lives with its hopes, fears, joys, and challenges and to get spiritual support and guidance from the group members.

Resources
Commentaries on the Rule for a general readership:
Joan Chittister, O.S.B., *The Rule of Benedict: Insight for the Ages*. I have often used this in groups.

Esther de Waal, *A Life-Giving Way: A Commentary on the Rule of St. Benedict*.

Norvene Vest, *Preferring Christ: A Devotional Commentary on the Rule of St. Benedict*.

Reflections on Benedictine spirituality:
Elizabeth J. Canham, *Heart Whispers: Benedictine Wisdom for Today*.

Joan Chittister, O.S.B., *Wisdom Distilled from the Daily*. I have often used this in groups.

Esther de Waal, *Seeking God: The Way of St. Benedict*.

Columba Stewart, *Prayer and Community: The Benedictine Tradition*.

Brian C. Taylor, *Spirituality for Everyday Living: An Adaptation of the Rule of St. Benedict.*

Jane Tomaine, *St. Benedict's Toolbox: The Nuts and Bolts of Everyday Benedictine Living.* I have often used this in groups.

Model 8:
Companions in Transition

> *God is our refuge and strength,*
> *a very present help in trouble.*
> *Therefore we will not fear, though the earth be moved,*
> *and though the mountains be toppled*
> *into the depths of the sea;*
> *Though its waters rage and foam,*
> *and though the mountains tremble at its tumult.*
> *The LORD of hosts is with us;*
> *the God of Jacob is our stronghold.*
> *—Psalm 46:1–4* [3]

Focus

Companions in Transition is an example of a group focused on providing a spiritual community for those who are facing similar challenges in their lives. In particular, *Companions in Transition* intends to provide spiritual support for those who desire a place where life-changing transitions can be explored in companionship with others who are also experiencing major change.

Background

This kind of group organizes around a similar life challenge affecting its members and offers spiritual resources to strengthen and assist them. The profound growth and lifesaving potential of Alcoholics Anonymous and other Twelve Step program groups attests to the power of receiving and sharing peer support and mutual guidance. Hospitals often sponsor care groups for those dealing with cancer or other life-threatening illnesses. Hospice organizations and sometimes churches provide bereavement groups to provide support, information, and guidance to grieving members. These, too, are part of this category of groups. Covenant groups (where there are promises of support and spiritual exploration together) for women's or men's spirituality benefit from this kind of group structure.

Group Form

The context for one particular covenant group I developed came from a recognition of the huge transitions that students, and often their loved ones and families, experience in moving to a residential seminary and beginning graduate-level study while also being expected to engage in high levels of seminary community involvement. Often they have ended a previous career and have thus moved from a social location of professional status (and high power) to the low status (and low power) of being a student. A house may have been sold, finances may be uncertain; their spouses and children also experience dislocation, or the student may be living in seminary alone, separated from spouse or family. Students often are facing graduate-level studies after being out of school for many years, and find the adjustment difficult. It is a scary and exciting time, and the stakes are high.

Paula Barker, the associate professor who was my field colleague and supervisor, suggested that entering students might benefit from a group designed to offer mutual support in their first few terms. I was grateful for the suggestion. When I was a first-year divinity student at Seabury in 1981, some of us entering students went to the administration and proposed that we have a group for personal and professional reflection and support with outside facilitation. We paid a small tuition fee and received a little credit. Our facilitator was a doctoral student in pastoral psychotherapy at Garrett-Evangelical Theological Seminary, Sister Joan Scanlon.[4] That weekly gathering of ten or so students with Joan's facilitation became a crucial support for me over the first few terms. So, to be able to offer something like that group to a new generation of students was personally gratifying.

Here is a general structure for *Companions in Transition* groups, based on the structure of our seminary group:

Companions in Transition
Group Process

1. Opening Ritual

2. Check-in
   An opportunity for group members to share how they are feeling, what has shaped them in this past week, etc. (20 minutes)

3. Engaging Scripture
   The leader selects a portion of sacred story related to call or journey for the group to sit with and explore. The leader might ask such questions as: What is similar and different in the story to our own stories? Who do we most identify with and/or feel most distant from? What is God like in the story? Who is God for us? Or

the leader might use a meditation exercise or another way of inviting members to engage the Scripture passage. (15 minutes)

[short break]

4. Engaging the Reading
   The leader invites members to look at the reading assigned for this session to use as a springboard/dialogue partner in exploring our lived experience of transition and life in seminary. (about 30 minutes)

5. Further Reflection arising from #2–4. (as time allows)

6. Closing Ritual

7. Process Review[5]

In our group we used both Scripture and contemporary writings as springboards to reflect on our own stories of dealing with major transition in our life, including the immediate seminary experience for the group members.

I put together some Scripture possibilities with themes of journey and call that the rotating group leaders might draw from. Since the students were in the middle of exploring their sense of vocational calling, and many were making physical journeys as well as interior spiritual journeys, exploring those themes using Scripture seemed helpful:

Journey and Call Themes in Scripture

+ Call of Abram, Abram and Sarai in Egypt (Gen. 12)

+ Covenant, birth of Ishmael (Gen. 15–16)

+ New name, son promised (Gen. 17–18)

+ Birth of Isaac, rejection of Hagar and Ishmael, sacrifice of Isaac (Gen. 21–22)

+ Jacob flees Esau, dream at Bethel (Gen. 27:41–28:22)

+ Jacob wrestles with angel, reconciliation with Esau (Gen. 32:22–33:20)

+ Moses at burning bush, receives mission (Exod. 3–4)

+ Pillar of cloud and fire, crossing Red Sea (Exod. 13:17–15:21)

+ Bitter water made sweet, bread from heaven (Exod. 15:22–16:21)

- Tablets of Covenant, golden calf, new tablets, shining face (Exod. 31:18–34:35)

- Complaints in desert, seventy elders (Num. 11:1–30)

- Spies to Canaan, people rebel (Num. 13, 14)

- Moses' death, Joshua takes over leadership (Deut. 34; Josh. 1:1–9)

- Ruth and Naomi (Book of Ruth)

- Beginning of Jesus' ministry (Mark 1)

- Jesus rejected, mission of the twelve (Mark 6:1–13)

- Women followers of Jesus (Luke 8:1–3)

- Would-be followers, mission of seventy, repentance (Luke 9:57–10:24)

- Triumphal entry to Jerusalem (Luke 19:28–48)

- Resurrection, Emmaus (Luke 24)

- Philip and Ethiopian eunuch (Acts 8:4–13, 26–40)

- Conversion of Saul (Acts 9:1–30)

- Paul's journey to Jerusalem (Acts 21:1–36)

I expect that most, if not all, religious faith traditions have Scripture or sacred stories that refer to the sense of divine call to humans, and the call into service, as well as the sense of sacred journey or pilgrimage. The idea is to help people tell their own stories and notice similarities and differences to the stories and poetry in their sacred traditions. In the Jewish and Christian traditions there is a major arc in sacred narrative that in Christianity we call the Paschal Mystery. I have graphed this as a way of presenting the path that transition and identity often take:

Personalizing the Paschal Mystery

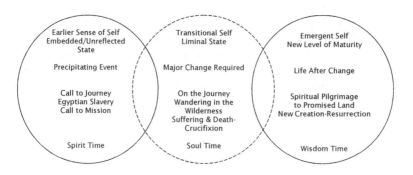

The intent of this graph is to give people a sense that there is a discernible pattern of movement in major transitions, and each of the states of selfhood can also identify with spiritual themes and religious stories. Regarding the times at the bottom of each sphere, I am drawing on some language that Bill Kauth and others have used to contrast "spirit" and "soul." The difference between these times can be illustrated below:[6]

Spirit and Soul Polarities

SPIRIT	SOUL
ascent	descent
non-material	material
known	unknown/confusion
clarity	mystery
detachment	attachment
light	dark
transcendent	immanent
universal	particular
perfection	imperfection
health	sickness
growth	decay
goal	obstacle/wander
success	failure
joy	sorrow
gain	loss
life	death

Let me relate these categories to the paradigm on transitional states. There can be a time when something erupts into a previously set life condition. For the Hebrew people in slavery in Egypt the previously known, established life condition was miserable (it was a soul time in many ways). The intervention of God's compassion and action, through Moses, initiated a spirit time, where there was suddenly a movement toward liberation. After the angel of death passed over the Hebrew slaves' homes, marked with the blood of a lamb on the lintel of the door, a new beginning was inaugurated with the Exodus from Egypt. The old self-identity, being a slave under oppression by Egyptians, began to be overturned. There was a new goal (freedom) and a new hope (a Promised Land) emerging. God called Moses to a mission that required the people to begin a journey, which had both physical and exterior as well as spiritual and interior dimensions.

In the Christian story the Jewish people under the rule of an occupying Roman force, with the corruption of some of the religious authorities, in a particular time and place experience God's intervention in the form of Jesus of Nazareth. Jesus understands himself as relating to God as his Father. He discerns a calling to a special mission and ministry and in turn assembles a band of disciples to follow him and participate with him in this spiritual mission of proclaiming and showing the in-breaking of the kingdom of God. This is a spirit time for himself and his followers.

As the Hebrew people move deeper into their journey, they confront new fears and resistances to the immense change that a movement toward liberation brings. They begin losing their old sense of identity but then find themselves unsure who they are and to whom they truly belong. This is a liminal state (a threshold experience) with all the ambiguity that comes with dealing with a future that is uncertain and a present situation that is anxious and challenging. They question their leaders and whether this God would truly provide for them in a harsh wilderness. Some want to go back to what they had known. Some want to worship the gods of their oppressors. They spend a generation wandering in the wilderness. This is symptomatic of a soul time.

Likewise, as Jesus deepens his ministry of healing, teaching, and other actions of compassion that are inaugurating the in-breaking of God's kingdom, he encounters resistance from various religious interests and confusion within his own band of followers. He is not the person some hoped he would be—he is not the imagined and hoped-for messiah who would overthrow Roman rule and reestablish a Davidic empire. In Jerusalem, near the time of the Passover celebration, Jesus holds his last supper with his disciples. He shares bread and wine, asking his followers to remember this as his body broken for them and his blood poured out for them. He becomes the paschal lamb in Christian symbolism. Then follow the betrayal, suffering, and crucifixion, with the disciples hiding out in terror. A soul time has reached its climax.

After forty years of wandering, the Israelites are shaped into a new people. They learn of God's faithful provision for their needs. They receive the Law and learn how to live in a new, disciplined way. Moses leads them up to the border of the Promised Land, but now authority is passed on to Joshua to take them to their new home. They have, through their trials and struggles and learning, been formed into a new identity. Their journey has taken them to a wisdom time that lends support for others in their own journeys through crisis, liminality, and new life.

So too in Christian experience, the resurrection of Jesus on the third day following his crucifixion inaugurates a new time and a new identity—a huge paradigm shift where death is overcome and new life is possible by God's grace and love. The gospel accounts vary, but encounters with the risen Christ are sometimes frightening (fears that he is a ghost; after all, it does shake up the known pattern of life and death), and sometimes he is not immediately recognized for who he truly is. Often he shows the wounds in his hands and side as a sign of who he is to his followers. So, the possibilities of living an Easter life or new life become part of the wisdom time for Christians.

In both these sacred stories, a new life and identity is forged through the integration of the spirit and soul events. Often in life wisdom emerges after we have gone through not only times of spirit but also times of soul. In fact, I would say that if our sacred stories and rites and community cannot hold us in *both* of those times in our own lives and lead us into a greater spiritual wisdom, they are worthless. This is the challenge of a group such as *Companions in Transition.*

In the *Companions in Transition* groups I have taught (*coached* is a more accurate term), I have used contemporary readings as well as Scripture reflection as springboards to sharing and support. There are plenty of books that can serve this purpose, and they might be selected with a particular kind of needed support in mind. In the case of the entering seminarians, I used two books for reflection and discussion: Parker Palmer's *Let Your Life Speak: Listening for the Voice of Vocation,* and Esther de Waal's slim little meditation on her movement into retirement, *To Pause at the Threshold: Reflections on Living on the Border.* Both of these authors provide a contemplative dimension to their writing and are undefended in their self-disclosures. They invited the kind of discussion and openness that I hoped the group's members could share.

One of the students who was in a *Companions in Transition* small group included the following statement in her reflection paper at the end of the course:

> As I traveled on this journey for thirteen weeks, I remembered that I initially thought it was unnecessary. However, as the weeks and group evolved I began to think that I could not do without them. There were critical times after a hard awakening in another class, my son's incarceration, and my sister's death that being a companion on the journey with others saved my psyche from spiraling into an abyss. The support provided returned a hope in me that I had lost many years ago.

Amidst the major transition work that occurs at times of change, such as the entrance into seminary and its intensive focus on vocational development, other events are likely to happen along the way that stretch our capacity to cope. It can be helpful to have a place and people to process the big and little things that life brings us. A group that can support us with faithful lovingkindness and a trust in God's care and grace for us, even when we cannot believe it ourselves, can make a big difference in how we go through the changes required of us.

Resources
Books or other materials to be used will depend on the nature of the transitions the group intends to support. Poetry, art, songs and chants, clay sculpturing, drawing, or movies that touch on a relevant theme can all be useful resources, too.

These groups are examples of small communities of spiritual support formed around a covenant relationship. The *Benedictine Community* group gives its members deep roots in a primary spiritual tradition. The *Companions in Transition* group holds the characteristic of compassion in common with the groups developed in the next chapter.

chapter six

Groups for Compassion and Social Action

LET'S TRY AN EXERCISE. Take a deep breath in and hold it for a moment. Then let it out with a full exhalation. Again, breathe in, hold it, and then exhale. Again, breathe in a full breath and hold it. . . . But what happens if you just breathe in and then hold on to it? So too our spiritual life is like that inhalation and exhalation pattern—that breathing in and breathing out. We are in trouble if we just breathe in, or just breathe out. I often like to pray a prayer of the heart where I breathe in the word *God* and breathe out the word *love*. I pray that my life is like that prayer—taking in and receiving the inner nourishment of God's Presence, being filled with the Spirit, and offering my embodiment of that Presence to the world around me in actions of love and compassionate service.

Any spiritual companionship group worth its salt is going to provide deep spiritual care and nurture of its members, but it will also equip them to be more compassionate people in a world that is in desperate need of loving actions of care, healing, reconciliation, and justice. The group forms its members to become deeper and more compassionate listeners—schooling us in the ability "to be with" (*com*) the "suffering" (*passion*). Our stance toward the world around us is shaped by the experiences we have of being able to give and receive loving attention to each other, and a spiritual companionship group's community dynamics contribute to such experiences. However, some groups may be designed for more direct action in the world. The two models presented in this chapter are examples of groups that have a *particular* mission of compassionate service and/or social action.

Model 9:
Healing Prayer

*O Lord my God, I cried out to you,
and you restored me to health.
You brought me up, O Lord, from the dead;
you restored my life as I was going down to the grave.*
—Psalm 30:2–3 [1]

Focus
The *Healing Prayer* group's purpose is to build the ministry of intercession and healing among its members and in the broader service of
the church and the world.

Background
Among the core theological underpinnings of small groups we have
already discussed are the God-movements toward shalom and wholeness. One of the signs of the in-breaking of the realm of the Divine is
healing. Whether it is the story of Elijah bringing the widow of
Zarephath's son back from death (1 Kings 17:17–24), or Elisha's healing
of Naaman from leprosy (2 Kings 5:1–19), or Jesus' healings throughout
his ministry, or the extension of that ministry through Jesus' disciples,
or the gathering of elders to pray and anoint with oil a sick person
(James 5:14), or in the vision of the trees whose leaves are for the healing of the nations (Rev. 22:2)—the testimony of Hebrew and Christian
Scripture is that healing can occur as a gift of God and a sign of the
Spirit's presence and work among us. And this movement toward healing and wholeness is multidimensional. It includes everything from the
recovery of health from disease or traumatic accident to inner healing
of painful memories and emotional distress, from movements through
grief and ministering to those dealing with mental or emotional illness
to supporting those who are struggling with addictions and working
toward the healing of our society and environment and relationships
in the global community.

In mainline churches the ministry of healing has often been approached with caution, probably rightly so, because of the possible exploitation of the most vulnerable of human beings by charlatans.
Images of televangelist hype come to my mind almost immediately
when I think of faith healing and possible exploitation. However, mainline churches ought to move beyond a reactive stance and claim the
importance of continuing Jesus' mission of healing and compassion to
broken, wounded, and suffering lives. People like Agnes Stanford and
Katherine Kuhlman in the mid-twentieth century did much to bring the
healing ministry into the Christian mainstream. In the 1960s the Roman

Catholic Church reaffirmed the ministry of healing prayer for the sick by extending the sacrament of Unction of the Sick beyond the practice of "last rites" to include prayers for healing. With the 1979 *Book of Common Prayer* the Episcopal Church likewise provided a sacramental rite for "anointing the sick with oil, or the laying on of hands, by which God's grace is given for the healing of spirit, mind, and body."[2] *The Book of Occasional Services* includes "A Public Service of Healing" that invites lay people with the gift of healing to participate along with the principal celebrant of the healing rite. That form extended the sacramental healing rite's administration to laity. Other denominations have likewise provided materials and forms for healing services to develop this healing ministry. And since the 1930s the Order of St. Luke the Physician has been an ecumenical and international resource for the Christian healing ministry.[3]

My own experience of the power of the church's ministry of healing prayer began as I visited a small healing prayer group in my church as a young adult. As I remember it, after an opening prayer the group sang some renewal-type songs from a tape recording, and then whoever wished to was welcome to come and kneel in center of the circle and state their healing concern. Members of the group gently laid hands on the head or shoulders of the person, and various members offered prayers for support and healing. After some time in prayer the group's members removed their hands and bid others to come to the center if they wished prayer for themselves or others. It was a fairly free-form structure that included one of the parish priests and some parishioners who were dedicated to that group's ministry. The group met regularly in the evening and visitors were welcome.

There was a year in my early thirties when I was going through the emotional anguish of marriage separation and divorce that I regularly went to a simple Friday noonday Eucharist at my church, which offered sacramental healing. That gentle and regular healing rite, alongside the understated power of the Eucharist, was a great comfort and source of support in a time of huge transition in my life. As a priest I have loved to help build and support the healing ministry of individuals and groups in churches, and I have witnessed healing on many levels, often slow and subtle but sometimes rather surprising and moving. My colleagues have also reported some of their own experiences of God's healing grace breaking through in profound ways—sometimes in the face of our own rationalistic, skeptical attitudes.

Group Form

When I was teaching at Seabury-Western Seminary I had the opportunity to hold several *Healing Prayer* group courses in the Spiritual Formation in Small Groups series. A primary text we used in that group was Avery Brooke's *Healing in the Landscape of Prayer.* I attended one of Avery's healing missions when I was a parish priest and found her to be well-grounded in history and theology as well as dedicated to building vital healing ministries.

An additional text we used was Flora Wuellner's *Prayer, Stress, and Our Inner Wounds.* I met Flora when I participated in the Academy for Spiritual Formation offered by The Upper Room. Her work as one of the faculty sensitized me to some of the ways church language can wound vulnerable people. Her depth prayer meditations were in accord with what I knew as profound ways of entering our spiritual being with God's grace.

We used the basic structure for groups with a few simple modifications, as described here.

Healing Prayer Group Process

1. Opening the Group
   Prayer, chant, lighting candle, or other simple action

2. Check-in
   Members share what they wish the group to know about them since the last meeting

3. Topical Exploration
   Using text, case example, or other focus for group discussion related to healing and spiritual life

4. Group Practice
   Intercessory prayer, litany, meditation, and/or healing ritual

5. Reflection and Process Review
   Sharing any thoughts about how the group is doing its work or what of significance has arisen for members in the practice

6. Closing the Group
   Prayer, sharing a word or image, or other simple action

Avery Brooke's *Healing in the Landscape of Prayer* is an excellent primer for getting a healing prayer group to look at some of the dynamics of prayer and healing. That book, or some similar resource, could be read in its entirety for discussion by all members in advance of starting a group healing ministry or for deepening an existing group's understanding. Ongoing study and reflection using a variety of sources can continue adding depth to the group's understanding of healing prayer and healing ministries (as in movement 3 above, Topical Exploration).

In one of our groups I asked members what questions they had as we looked at scriptural stories of healing. They came up with a wonderful list that would be great for topical discussions and reflection:

1. Why is there a difference between the centrality of healing in Jesus' ministry and the church's healing ministry practice?

2. Have we distanced ourselves from healing? (What are the barriers?)

3. What does Jesus mean by this healing business?

4. If we believe in healing, what are our faith implications?

5. Is healing a free gift or are we supposed to do something in response?

6. What does Jesus mean by "your faith has made you well"?

7. What is behind stories of some women's automatic response of service, some men's rejoicing and proclamation, and other people simply being healed without particular response?

8. Can actions of healing bring on reprisal from religious authorities and established church leaders like the resistance to some of Jesus' healings?

9. Why does touch, physical contact, seem to be a primary element of many healing stories?

10. What role does intention play in healing (both human and divine intention)?

11. Why do the biblical healing stories nearly always get reported as instantaneous, rather than progressive? (An exception is the two-stage healing of the blind man who first sees people like trees, and then gets a second touch.)

12. Does healing always equal cure?

At the beginning of the group's life there may be a desire to explore a variety of practices (movement 4). I encourage the group to focus its healing practices on its own members first, as well as offering prayer intercessions from the members. Later the group members can explore whether to invite others to their sessions if they are wishing healing prayer, or if they are to use this as a foundational base for members offering healing ministries outside the group.

An example of a group practice is this simple guided imagery meditation, *Meeting the Healer,* an adaptation of the meditation on *Meeting the Inner Wise One* in the section in chapter 3 on the *Circle of the Spirit* groups. Jungians would say that the Wise One and Healer are two archetypes that we have within and can engage. Just because we might call them archetypes does not mean that they cannot be divine energies used by God for giving us wisdom and guidance or healing and direction toward greater wholeness.

Meeting the Inner Healer

- Close your eyes, if you are comfortable doing so, and take a few slow, full, cleansing breaths in and out.

- Imagine you are in a green meadow.

- Look around and notice what you see and feel and smell. Notice how the ground feels beneath your feet.

- Notice that there is a narrow dirt path that leads up a small hill. Take a walk on that path, up the hill, to the place where the Healer stays.

- When you reach the door to the house of the Healer, knock at the door and enter when you are invited to do so.

- Look around the room and look at the Healer. What do you see in the room? Who or what does the Healer look like to you? Are there others in the room?

- You may have a question for the Healer or you might wish to tell the Healer about something that you are now considering. Ask the Healer's counsel on whatever you wish, and listen for his or her reply. If you need clarification feel free to engage in further conversation with the Healer.

- The Healer says that she or he has something for you. It might be a special word or phrase, an object, a song, a healing touch, a prayer, or some other gift. Receive the gift the Healer has for you, and feel free to ask about it if you need to know more. Respond to the Healer's gift in whatever way you think is appropriate.

- It is now time to say farewell to the Healer. Say your goodbye in whatever way you feel is appropriate, and then go to the door... walk down the hill on the path... and to the meadow,... remembering your time with the Healer and the gift you received, knowing also that you can visit your inner Healer again. Whenever you are ready, open your eyes and bring your attention back to the group.

It is important to raise the issue of healing from spiritual oppression and deliverance ministries, although I will not be able to give it as thorough a conversation as it deserves. In mainline church circles we rarely have discussions about the need for deliverance ministry, but instead have tended to avoid it as superstitious manipulation of the psyche and leave it to churches and groups more strongly influenced by Pentecostal or charismatic influence. When I have had *Healing Prayer* groups at the seminary I found students hungry to explore the topic and frustrated by the lack of pastoral discussions around issues of demonic influence. I think that in being afraid to raise the topic for fear of sensationalism, or by calling all situations solely a mental health issue and not inviting opportunities to hear people's experiences, we fail to provide important healing resources for the people in our spiritual care.

In the Episcopal Church there is hardly anything in our publicly available liturgical resources about deliverance from demonic influence. In the *Book of Common Prayer,* the closest we get to a specific prayer for protection and cleansing of demonic forces is in the nighttime service of Compline:

> Visit this place, O Lord, and drive far from it all snares of the enemy; let your holy angels dwell with us to preserve us in peace; and let your blessing be upon us always; through Jesus Christ our Lord. *Amen.*[4]

Also in the *Book of Common Prayer* is a healing rite that includes a prayer that the priest may say while laying on hands (and optionally anointing with oil):

> *N.,* I lay my hands upon you in the Name of the Father, and of the Son, and of the Holy Spirit, beseeching our Lord Jesus Christ to sustain you with his presence, to drive away all sickness of body and spirit, and to give you that victory of life and peace which will enable you to serve him both now and evermore. *Amen.*[5]

Neither this prayer nor the prayer in Compline directly uses language addressing oppressive spirits as the source of snares or sickness. In the baptismal liturgy the candidate is asked to renounce "Satan and all the spiritual forces of wickedness that rebel against God," "the evil powers of this world which corrupt and destroy the creatures of God," and "all sinful desires that draw you from the love of God."[6]

In the supplemental *Book of Occasional Services,* a service of house blessing includes a prayer that may be said for cleansing from evil:

> Let the mighty power of the Holy God be present in this place to banish from it every unclean spirit, to cleanse it from every residue

of evil, and to make it a secure habitation for those who dwell in it; in the Name of Jesus Christ our Lord. *Amen.*[7]

Sometimes holy water and/or incense is used in the various rooms as ritual actions of purification and sanctification. *The Book of Occasional Services* also simply directs people who feel they need the help of exorcism to contact their bishop. No priest is authorized to conduct an exorcism except with the direct permission of the bishop.[8]

Helpful to any mainstream exploration of a healing ministry that might address questions of deliverance is Avery Brooke's *Healing in the Landscape of Prayer.* Another resource is the book *Deliverance* by the Church of England's Exorcism Study Group and edited by Michael Perry. Beginning in 1974 the Church of England established in each diocese an exorcism or deliverance ministry team usually composed of a designated and trained priest and mental health professionals. The approach of the team, often using *Deliverance* as its basic resource, is deeply pastoral, and members of the team may be agnostic about the actual existence of demonic spirits and causes of paranormal activity. Celebration of the Holy Eucharist is often part of the ritual practice used for deliverance and restoration to health.[9]

Resources

Avery Brooke, *Healing in the Landscape of Prayer.* A great introduction to the Christian ministry of healing prayer and developing a healing prayer group.

Dwight H. Judy, *Christian Meditation and Inner Healing.* Offers psychological depth and theological understanding to the topic of inner healing. Comments about a group process are included.

Morton Kelsey, *Healing and Christianity: A Classic Study.* Another big historical study by Kelsey with his own theories of the inner spiritual world drawn from his Jungian understandings.

Bobbie McKay and Lewis A. Musil, *Healing the Spirit: Stories of Transformation.* The authors did a wonderful study of mainline Protestant congregations in recent years and share many stories of healing told by those they surveyed. We need to hear these stories.

Agnes Sanford, *The Healing Light.* Classic 1947 work on Christian healing prayer.

Flora Slosson Wuellner, *Prayer, Stress, and Our Inner Wounds.* Flora has written a number of books similar to this one.

Model 10:
Covenant for Justice and Peace

> And what does the LORD quire of you?
> To act justly and to love mercy
> and to walk humbly with your God.
> —Micah 6:8b (NIV)

Focus

The *Covenant for Justice and Peace* group is committed to critical social analysis, spiritual reflection, and action for justice and peace in the members' lives, communities, and world.

Background

In the Episcopal Church questions are asked of everyone whenever a baptism is celebrated and on other special days when the members of the community renew their Baptismal Covenant:

Will you seek and serve Christ in all persons, loving your neighbor as yourself?

Will you strive for justice and peace among all people, and respect the dignity of every human being?

The community responds to each of these questions: "I will, with God's help."[10]

Whether formally acknowledged as part of the covenant that is central to being members of the church or expressed in a multitude of other ways less formally defined, active faith and spirituality demands ethical and compassionate treatment of all people and critical engagement with the social structures that affect people's well-being. Jewish law requires care of the stranger, the widow, and others who are on the margins of society. The prophets roundly condemned actions of injustice and oppression of the needy and poor—warning of God's divine judgment against such misuse of power and authority. Jesus put love of God, neighbor, and self as the three dimensions that summarized the Law. In Matthew 25 the judgment of the nations is based on whether or not they have shown care for the hungry, the thirsty, the stranger, the naked, the sick, and the prisoner. This judgment carries a profound message on the incarnational presence, for the Divine King himself was secretly present in the ones who needed the care.

In the twentieth and twenty-first centuries, the social gospel movement and liberation theologies are manifestations of faith-informed social critique and action. Dorothy Day and the Catholic Worker movement formed a powerful witness and articulated a Christian identification with the poor. The Reverend Martin Luther King, Jr., garnered support from many people of faith in the struggle for civil rights and the efforts to dismantle structural and systemic racism in the United States. Feminist theology and the feminist movement brought critical reflection and action on women's liberation. The gay liberation movement began advocating for lesbian, gay, bisexual, and transgender people's freedom from discrimination and violence against those with a sexual orientation different from the heterosexual majority. None of these movements has completed their work, for oppression and discrimination still are entrenched in our social structures, and people of faith are not of one mind on many issues. Adding to these and other important human rights and welfare concerns, there are major ecological considerations as well as global policy issues of economic justice and the limits of military involvement.[11]

In the 1970s to early 1980s, I worked for the Michigan Department of Social Services, first as a child care services worker in an east-side district in Detroit and later in quality assurance investigations as part of the state office's field staff. This work opened my eyes to the poverty traps that people without privilege are forced into by a social system designed to maintain unequal benefits and privileges based on race and social status. I saw not only the anger and frustration and hopelessness of many people caught in that trap—but also the soul-exhausting impact on social services workers and caseworkers who are on the front line of trying to deliver help and assistance. I saw a significant number of workers turn to drugs, cynicism, and hardness of heart to numb themselves from the demoralizing effects of the system that they were co-opted into. Some experienced mental or emotional illness, and a few used the system for their own corrupt personal gain. I was not set apart from those workers who coped badly. For most of the years I worked in social services I had an insufficient spiritual foundation to support myself in a healthy way. Since the time that I went through a spiritual reawakening and later entered ordained ministry, it has been my objective to help provide spiritually supportive communities for those who feel the demoralizing effects of a system of privilege stacked against them, for those who work to deliver needed assistance, and for those who are laboring to effect systemic change.

Unfortunately, we often have poor theology to contend with alongside an entrenched system of discrimination, racism, and unequal privilege. Robert McAfee Brown called it the "Great Fallacy."[12] Although spirituality and efforts of liberation are actually two sides of the same thing, poor theology separates them and develops a hierarchy. The spiritual is seen as separate from and more important than that which is material. That split causes all kinds of havoc. It relegates spirituality to the realm of "heavenly minded and no earthly good." It cuts social reformers and activists off from the divine foundation and source of energy for their sustained efforts. It is the kind of fallacy that caused Karl Marx to criticize religion as the opiate of the people, or Sigmund Freud to see religion as nothing more than projected fantasy. For spiritual health and the health of the world, we must challenge this fallacy and provide groups that support the unity of spiritual growth and social reform. An incarnational and sacramental theology does just that.

Group Form

Just as there is no one true spiritual path for everybody, so there is no one way that our spiritual lives will be expressed in actions of compassion, justice-making, and peace. The *Covenant for Justice and Peace* group commits to supporting members in their desire to bring spirituality and justice together in their lives in a variety of ways. For an ongoing group I prefer to have an organizational meeting before actually starting a group session in order to get the members to agree on a basic covenant and how they wish to shape their group's focus.

A basic covenant includes their agreement on how members will conduct themselves in conversation and sharing of perspectives (we will go into that more in discussion about a Foundations document in chapter 7), whether there is outside study involved, and what kind of support they can expect from each other outside of group time. There are a number of ways that members shape their focus. For example, everyone could agree to take turns bringing to the group a critical incident or situation they are dealing with that involves a justice and peace theme. This kind of group will likely go deeply into the personal lives of members, supporting them in their struggles to act creatively and courageously in the particular situations life is presenting to them. Another group might be interested in focusing on a single issue and structure time devoted to study, discussion, and application. This would be a good method for an advocacy/action group such as a local chapter of a faith-based peacemaking organization like the Episcopal Peace Fellowship or Pax Christi, or a group focused on dismantling racism, especially if there is a desire for the group as a whole to initiate actions. Alternatively, members might rotate presenting an issue of their own choice for group focus and discussion. This would be particularly useful if the group sees its purpose as consciousness-raising.

Once the organizational meeting establishes the group's particular means of engaging the subject of justice and peace and adopts a basic covenant, the group is ready to hold its sessions. Here's an example of how this group might be structured:

Covenant for Justice and Peace Group Process

1. Prayer and Spiritual Centering

2. Check-in: including personal justice and peace issues

3. Presentation/Slice of Life (focus)*

4. Personal/Communal Exploration of Justice and Peace Issues*

5. Application as Individuals and/or Group or Parish Life in this Time*

6. Process Review

Informed by Scripture, reason, and tradition

Please note that in the check-in time, members of a *Covenant for Justice and Peace* group are given the opportunity briefly to report in on any justice/peace issues that have arisen for them in the week, as well as the usual check-in possibilities. This also sets the stage for a designated member to present to the group a slice-of-life issue that occurred during the week for the group to explore during the session. It is usually helpful for the group's facilitation leader to be different from the presenter. This structure has fluid movements, from a presenter's case situation to an exploration of issues that the case generates, to a consideration of possible invitations of God to the individuals or the group as a whole for action or application. Throughout these movements, the group will need to be open to considering how Scripture, reason, and tradition might inform them.

In order to assist members in their approach to the critical incident/case study, I have developed a reflection process to help guide the discussion:

A Case Study / Critical Incident
Reflection Process

Here are some guiding questions to consider in working with a case situation:

1. Describe the event/incident related to the subject of striving for justice, peace, and respecting the dignity of every human being:
   What happened?
   What was the context in which this occurred?
   What occurred within you? (How did you feel? What was evoked?)
   Did you or others do anything after the situation occurred?

2. What questions or topics emerged that you would like to explore?

3. Is there anything in particular that you want or need from the group?

4. Some group reflection possibilities:
   What occurred within us as we heard the situation?
   (Feelings, thoughts, images, parallel experiences?)
   Do Scripture texts or stories or images come to mind?
   Does anything from our Christian spiritual tradition (liturgy, theology, saints, prayers, wisdom sayings, etc.) come to mind?
   Theologically, what does this say about our human condition and the nature of God, and about such topics as sin, grace, repentance, healing, forgiveness, reconciliation, empowerment?

5. Is there some invitation or call that God is giving us from these reflections?

As mentioned before, *Covenant for Justice and Peace* groups can organize in different ways. One group rotated topical interests, with a presenter giving a ripped-from-the-headlines article or Web download. The presenter also guided us in engaging Scripture and theological considerations for discussion. One group focused on racism and we did a read-through on a book with discussion, along with a personal story related to an incident involving racial discrimination. Since discrimination touches on other categories as well, stories started emerging from women about the pain of discrimination and from gay and lesbian members on some of their struggles.

One way of engaging Scripture for reflection and guidance in social change emerged from the Christian base communities in Central and South America.[13] Sometimes we would use this particular method, or an adaptation of it, in our group work:

Base Community Method of Bible Study

Ask a group member to read the passage.

1. Invite the group to discuss the political, social, and historical context of the text. Group members may want to read what comes before and after the text, look at a study Bible, or consult a commentary.

2. Invite the group to listen to the text again with the context in mind; ask a different group member to reread the passage.

3. Invite members to share comments and reflections on the text.

4. Invite the group to identify the similarities and differences between the world of the text and their world.

5. Invite group members to identify the problems and issues in their common life which are raised by the discussion of the text. These problems should be ones shared by group members—issues in the neighborhood, community, region—rather than personal issues. Because this method calls a group to a common action, the group needs to identify common issues and concerns.

6. Ask how the text may be relevant to the group's reality. What does the text say to the group's issues, to the ways they are now responding to those issues, to the role of the church in response to those issues?

7. Invite the group to spend some time in prayer, seeking God's guidance.

8. Invite the group to decide what action they will take in the problem area discussed. Set a time for follow-up so the group can report what has happened as a result of the action taken. If this is an ongoing group, do this report time before starting study of the next passage.[14]

Group leaders may offer a guided meditation on either a Scripture story or imagining Christ present and engage in dialogue around a situation or concern. Journaling or an imaginative meditation with a leader in social change or compassionate action (Martin Luther King, Jr., Dorothy Day, César Chávez, Mother Teresa of Calcutta, Desmond Tutu, Mohandas Gandhi) is also a way to engage this group. The following is an example that I created for a group exercise:

In Dialogue with a Worker for Justice

1. If you could be in conversation with anyone from the past or present who has been a great leader in bringing about a more just world, who would that be? Who is someone you admire that has worked for justice or peace?

2. Imagine that you are walking on a path to the house where that person lives.

3. Notice what that area looks like. Go up to the door and knock.

4. This person has been expecting you, so he or she opens the door for you and welcomes you inside. You are invited to sit down on a chair next to that person to talk to him or her about whatever is on

your mind. Feel free to ask any questions you wish, and listen for the responses.

5. The worker for justice may have some questions for you, too. Answer honestly.

6. The worker for justice may have something for you ... a word of guidance or support for you ... a blessing ... a prayer for you ... or a symbolic object. Receive whatever is given to you.

7. Then say goodbye and when you exit the door, come back to consciousness of your normal life while bringing back the memory of this encounter with a great worker for social justice.

We also have made field trips in *Covenant for Justice and Peace* groups. One session coincided with a display of the *Christa* sculpture in the lobby of Garrett-Evangelical Theological Seminary, so we walked across the street to sit quietly with the sculpture for about twenty minutes. *Christa* is a powerful sculpture of a nude female Christ figure on a cross. Then we went to a quiet area outside the building to process some of our thoughts and feelings. The stories it evoked from a woman in the group and the level of sharing this experience generated were deeply profound. Another time we walked to the grounds of Evanston's Civic Center. On the grounds is an Avenue of the Righteous memorial dedicated by Jewish members of the community in recognition of Gentiles who risked their lives helping Jews escape from Nazi oppression and the Holocaust. Visits such as these add a powerful dimension to the group's life and support of social justice and peacemaking efforts.

Resources

Robert McAfee Brown, *Spirituality and Liberation: Overcoming the Great Fallacy*. Although the way Brown's argument is laid out makes this book a difficult read, it is worth going through it. I especially appreciated his work with liberation theologians and his treatment of incarnational theology.

Curtiss Paul DeYoung, *Living Faith: How Faith Inspires Social Justice*. This book provides biographies of many famous social justice leaders from various faith traditions.

Katherine Marie Dyckman, S.N.J.M., and L. Patrick Carroll, S.J., *Inviting the Mystic, Supporting the Prophet: An Introduction to Spiritual Direction*. The authors introduce the art of spiritual direction with this title focus in mind. Well worth reading for leaders of justice and peace groups.

Susan Rakoczy, I.H.M., *Great Mystics and Social Justice: Walking on the Two Feet of Love*. Another book that provides a platform for discussion drawing on the lives of mystics from biblical and early Christianity up to contemporary figures like Desmond Tutu and Nelson Mandela.

Carolyn Schrock-Shenk and Lawrence Ressler, eds., *Making Peace with Conflict: Practical Skills for Conflict Transformation*. This is a fine introduction to issues of conflict and peacemaking and a helpful approach to conflict transformation, written by Mennonites who have done a lot of work and education in this field.

Walter Wink wrote a series of books collectively called *The Powers Trilogy*. He subsequently published a book that is a synthesis and synopsis of the trilogy, *The Powers That Be: Theology for a New Millennium*. I appreciate his scholarship in explicating the meaning of scriptural words like *powers, principalities, angels,* and *demons* and in exploring modern meanings. His thesis on the domination system, discernment of the spirit/angel of a group, and nonviolent action is worthy of consideration.

Claire E. Wolfteich, *Lord, Have Mercy: Praying for Justice with Conviction and Humility*. This book is part of the excellent *Practices of Faith* series edited by Dorothy Bass. It provides background for fruitful conversations and exploring ways of praying in the midst of the struggle for justice.

In this chapter we have explored a few possibilities related to having groups that provide spiritual companionship with a focus on actions of compassion and social justice. These groups give members a solid spiritual foundation for such actions. This chapter also concludes the introduction to the basic models of spiritual companionship groups. Now we will consider issues related to the actual leadership of these kinds of groups.

chapter seven

Leading a
Small Group

WHEN I FINISHED piloting a spiritual companionship group leaders' training program for the Institute of Spiritual Companionship in the Chicago area, the Institute's leadership invited me to reflect with them on training essentials. One of the topics that emerged in our meeting was the role of a spiritual companionship group leader. We came up with the following list of tasks a leader should be prepared to undertake.

The Leader's Role

1. Determine the leadership structure: single leader, team, mentor and apprentice, rotation with coaching. (This could change over the life of the group.)

2. Oversee selection of potential group members.

3. Articulate the purpose of the group and provide an orientation to content and process for potential members.

4. Lead the group to formulate a consensus about its foundations (core principles for communication and expectations of one another).

5. Provide a non-anxious presence and clarity in early sessions while members are getting familiar with the process and content of the group.

6. Assist the group in periodically reviewing its work and making necessary or desired changes.

7. Be on the lookout for other potential leaders who might be encouraged.

8. Help the group recognize that members may have differing learning styles, and encourage exploring various modes for understanding.

9. Provide a process that respects healthy differences, allows for disagreement and creative outcomes, and yet is able appropriately and respectfully to confront dysfunctional behavior.

10. Advocate by word and deed for the well-being of the individual members and the group as a whole, serving as a role model for all group members.

11. Support members and the group as a whole in working with discernment questions.

12. Be aware of stages in the life cycle of a group, and either lead the group through its life or provide guidance for selection of leaders appropriate for different stages.

13. Make use of regular consultative support and supervision outside the group.

14. Give appropriate attention to practical arrangements.

15. Be familiar with family systems and aware of helpful and unhelpful triangles.[1]

Establishing the Foundations

It takes careful planning and forethought to get a spiritual companionship group up and running. What is the platform for this group? Is it a church or an institution? If so, determine with whom you need to consult and what decision-making process you need to follow within the organization to get active approval and support. Discuss how the group fits within the overall structure and mission of the organization so there is agreement about how the group serves the purposes of the host organization. A church or organization does well to strategize deliberately about how to create small groups, including spiritual companionship groups, and the purpose these groups serve.

Some churches see themselves as a community *of* small groups. This is the vision articulated in the literature of some megachurches, for example, Willow Creek Community Church. In this view people need small groups to provide a sense of primary community where they are known by other group members, while they also participate in large gatherings for worship. Small groups are the building blocks of these churches. Other churches see themselves as a faith community that *has* small groups. Small groups here also provide an important primary community function, but groups are more likely seen as supportive and supplemental to the work of the whole church.

Selection of people for a spiritual companionship group is another important consideration. Not everyone is going to be happy and fit into this kind of group. Potential members need to have certain capacities that help spiritual companionship groups function well, such as:

♦ self-awareness

♦ ability to listen deeply and sensitively to others

♦ ability to respect privacy and keep sensitive information confidential

♦ ability to be comfortable with silence

♦ ability to engage both left- and right-brain processing

♦ respect for the work of the Holy Mystery within and among each other

♦ not dogmatically rigid or judgmental

♦ not too anxious or in need of more support than the group can reasonably provide

♦ not domineering or having a project of fixing or rescuing other people

♦ ability to both give to the group and receive from the group

♦ commitment to the group's process.

Members may find receiving individual spiritual direction beneficial alongside the group's companionship. Leaders would benefit from receiving personal or group spiritual direction prior to facilitating these kinds of groups.

It is helpful to offer an information session with a simple demonstration of the group for those who may be interested in joining. Discuss with leaders of the church/institution who might be prospective group members and if possible invite them personally to the information session. If an open invitation to everyone is given, the information session can help you assess potential members as well as give attendees a chance to assess how this kind of group matches their interests. Interviewing those who may be interested in a group before they join can help a leader discern suitability of candidates for group member-ship.

Ground Rules and Expectations

I prefer to go over basic expectations and ground rules for the group during an information meeting and then have that reaffirmed at the opening session of the new group. Over the years, I have developed a list of those rules and expectations that I refer to as the Foundations for the group and frame them as a group covenant. The Foundations can be modified by a consensus of the group's members at the opening session or at later times in the life of the group. I use this document as a template for spiritual companionship groups:

Foundations for a Spiritual Companionship Group

- ◆ Sacred hospitality is a hallmark of this group, practicing openness to the mystery of the Presence within ourselves and each other, and supporting our common desire to know that Presence.

- ◆ This group welcomes people of differing faiths, ages, genders, cultures, races, and sexual orientations and sees diversity as part of the richness of the group.

- ◆ There is great collective wisdom in this group.

- ◆ All are encouraged to speak in the group and to take the risk of sharing their reflections.

- ◆ We use "I" statements whenever possible. We try to own our statements from our personal experience, rather than speaking in generalities or on behalf of others.

- ◆ Everyone is encouraged to listen respectfully and refrain from dominating conversation.

- ◆ We respect members' basic need for confidentiality and trust building since sensitive issues might be explored.

- ◆ We arrive on time, start on time, end on time.

- ◆ We make the meetings a priority on our schedules. Our presence or absence affects the group.

Certain statements from this template will need to be modified given a particular group's context. For instance, if the group is for women or men only, or intended for seniors or young adults, the second statement will need modification. However, there could still be an emphasis on valuing diversity within the group as a gift. Most of the expectations are applicable to any of the groups described in this book. Group members may want to add statements to this Foundations covenant. They may want to have members commit to praying for one another between sessions. Members may want to suggest statements such as "We have fun together," or "Laughter and tears are welcome here." Sometimes a group wants greater accountability by adding a statement like "If a member is going to be absent he or she will let another member know in advance of the session." The modifications can be suggested by a member and discussed to see whether the whole group is agreeable to them.

An alternative is to ask the group members what they feel is needed in a commitment to each other to help the group be its very best and accomplish the intentions of the group. Then list their contributions to a group covenant and seek consensus about commitment. You can keep the Foundations in mind while the group is crafting their covenant and make suggestions if you feel that something important is being left out. This process of fashioning a covenant from the members' thoughts creates a strong sense of group ownership of the final product.

There is a great advantage in being clear from the beginning how the group is going to conduct itself, what behavior is encouraged, and what is not allowed from members. Making the norms clear and open rather than non-verbal and inferred establishes a level of accountability that may save the group uncomfortable anxiety and hard feelings later. There is security in knowing what is expected of each other.

Organizing the Group

Often it is helpful to have an organizational meeting of group members to discuss and negotiate various aspects of the group's life before actually starting the group. Or, the leader may arrange an extra hour or so at the beginning to discuss the group's organization and reach decisions. A number of organizational factors might be considered by the members:

Structure and Time Frame

How frequently will the group meet and how long will a session last? What is a reasonable structure within the time frame that is set? For instance, a *Holy Reading* group might decide to meet for forty-five minutes between church services every Sunday during Lent. There may be time for a brief check-in, but it will have to be carefully limited if there are six to eight group members. It might be agreed that the session will simply open by ringing a bell and the group will close by saying the Lord's Prayer together in a circle after each person gives a one-sentence word of encouragement to the member on their right side. But a *Dreamwork* group might decide to meet on the first and third Wednesday night of each month for a year from 7:00 p.m. until 9:30 p.m. at a host location, giving ample time for each movement in the evening's session.

Open or Closed Group?

The group needs to decide at the beginning whether it is to be open or closed to new members and visitors. An open group may have people come in and out, some as visitors and some who may want to join the group more formally. There are advantages to an open group in that new potential members have ready access to the group. An open group is also more transparent to the larger social system/community, and that provides a greater sense of accountability and scrutiny. However, it is harder to do consistent depth work in an open group. With new people visiting or being incorporated, some of the energy goes to attending to them and the trust level can be lessened. With a closed group, trust can be more quickly established and the group needn't expend time and energy with visitors and initiating new members. But a closed group can become stale or feel out of touch with the larger community. Some groups decide to be closed for a period of time and then open to new members, or when there is a critical mass they subdivide into several groups containing some experienced members and some new members.

Who Leads?

Another starting decision is who will lead the group. Is the group going to be facilitated by one person, or by several members, or by rotation of leadership among all of the members? It is not uncommon to have a single facilitator for an initial period of sessions as the group is getting its bearings. Groups tend to be more anxious at the beginning, and this often calls for a stronger leadership style at first. But once a group has gained some experience and internalized the movements it undergoes in a session, there may be interest in sharing the leadership role among members. Attentiveness to those who are showing leadership qualities suitable for spiritual companionship groups is an important strategy for growth of small groups. Again, there can be strategies developed for using new leaders, such as having them apprentice with the group leader or be a co-leader for a time, and then become the leader of a new group.

Process Reviews

When beginning a group there should be discussion and a decision on how frequently there will be a process review. My experience is that when this is institutionalized as a regular part of a meeting or set up on a periodic basis, the group will function more smoothly. Referring to the Foundations covenant can be an effective way for the group to

118

reflect how well it is doing the work it is committed to doing, and how well members are contributing in a healthy way to the community's life. Other questions can be asked for group reflection such as:

1. Did we notice times when the Divine seemed particularly present or where spiritual movement seemed blocked?

2. How well did we do our work together?

3. Were there any times when we got off-track?

4. Did we move into fixing or advice-giving?

5. Did the rhythm of the session seem right, or did we spend too much time in one part of our meeting?

6. How might we improve the way we are a group together?

7. Do we need to modify our Foundations covenant or change the group in any way?

Process reviews give us a chance to think about the life and health of the group, the way the members affect the group, and the way the group affects the members' lives. In the dominant American and Western European culture, much emphasis is placed on the individual. But here we need to also think of the group as a living organism. Certainly a group functions to support the spiritual lives of its individual members, but the group also has its own spiritual and emotional life. Leaders of companionship groups attend to the health of both its members and the group as a whole.

Leading a Group

Behavioral Interventions

Sometimes the group leader needs to intervene. A member might be reticent to contribute and needs to be invited to do so. Another group member unconsciously tends to dominate the conversation and needs to be reminded gently that others are due to speak. Sometimes someone is having a particularly hard time and needs a little more attention. Is this a time to ask the group if it is willing to modify the session's work a bit or just allow the wisdom of the group to handle the situation? Usually the leader should go gently into any intervention. Sometimes you might see a pattern develop that could be brought to the member's attention during a break or after a session. If someone seems to need more support than the group can provide, checking in with that person outside the meeting can be effective. Showing concern and asking about what resources the person has available is a responsible pastoral intervention. It is important to be able to refer a person who might benefit from professional psychotherapeutic or counseling help, pastoral care, or personal spiritual direction.

The group can also monitor the behavior of its members. If someone needs to be drawn out or someone is dominating the time, a healthy group takes responsibility for intervening rather than depending on the leader to take the initiative. Again, usually a gentle approach is best. Often pointing out a behavior and stating the feeling it elicited is helpful. "When you said/did..., I felt...." Or describing the behavior that you saw and asking the member if that is what was intended gives the person an opportunity to respond in a less defended way. The purpose of an intervention is to point out a behavior that is not helpful in the group, but it should not judge the person's worth to the group. A regular process review monitors how well the members, and the group as an entity, are adhering to their Foundations guidelines. Additionally, it encourages reflection on what helped or hindered the group's communication and sense of community.

The following are behaviors that can hinder healthy group life:

1. *Aggressor:* Deflates status of others; expresses disapproval of status, values, or acts of others; attacks the group or the problem it is working on.

2. *Blocker:* Negative, stubbornly resistant, or unreasonably disagreeable; attempts to maintain or rehash an issue the group has rejected.

3. *Recognition-seeker:* Often calls attention to self—boasting, reporting personal achievements, etc.

4. *Dominator:* Asserts self in authoritarian or superior manner to manipulate group or certain group members by using flattery, giving directions, interrupting others, etc.

5. *Band-aider:* Wants to fix things or persons without going through a healing process.

6. *Game Player:* Exhibits lack of involvement in the group's processes through horseplay, cynicism, or nonchalance; will not be real with the group.

7. *Unzipper:* Does not understand the difference between being open and being unzipped—in regards to self and/or others.[2]

While it is usually sufficient to point out gently to the person the behavior in question, there are times when a more direct challenge to a member's behavior is needed. An individual or two can hijack the good work of a group, subverting its dynamics and distorting its purposes. In one clergy group a person occasionally dropped in drunk and disruptive while a meeting was already well underway. After confronting his behavior several times, the group eventually needed to tell him that he was not welcome, that his behavior was disruptive and harmful to the group. We had to draw a line and advocate in favor of the health of the group. Our clergy brother clearly had severe problems but it was not our responsibility as a group to suspend our purpose for gathering and put all our energy into attempting to rescue him—which he did not want.

In another situation I felt it necessary to bar a person from participating in small groups for spiritual formation courses. That particular student, who was taking occasional courses for non-degree personal study, was not capable of engaging the group in any way other than as an academic exercise. I made attempts, in and outside of group sessions, to coach him on how to relate to others as a member of the group. Finally, I discussed with him, outside the group session, ways that might be more fruitful for his desire to study spirituality—a personal spiritual director, academic studies, or directed readings. But he needed to know that the small-group courses were not a good match for the way he studied and made contributions.

Sometimes the group as a whole can get off task. Wilfred Bion, an early leader in the study of group dynamics, and the Tavistock Institute have identified unconscious behaviors in group life that allow the group to avoid getting its tasks done. *Fight or flight* behavior may happen when the group feels anxious. The group might engage in *scapegoating* behavior as a way unconsciously to displace their anger and anxiety onto a member or an outside target. *Pairing* behavior occurs when a subgroup of two or more disengages its attention from the group by whispering or joking with each other, or forms a romantic relationship that can displace the emotional attention of the whole group. And *dependency* on the leader can be an unconscious tactic for the group to avoid responsibility for owning all members' responsibility for getting the work done effectively. The leader's responsibility with such nonfunctional behavior is to bring the behavior to the group's attention and let the group assume responsibility for changing it.

Decisions and Conflict

Let's face it. Get a few folks together for a while and some disagreements are bound to happen. It is normal to have some conflicts along the way. We have different perspectives, an intrinsic part of being limited human beings, which gives a richness to our groups and also brings with it tensions. Those places of disagreement and differing perspective can be the source of new creative thinking. Unfortunately

121

many of us have been wounded at some time or other in conflicts that were experienced as primarily destructive.

It is important for group leaders to handle the conflicts that are likely to arise with a sense of humility, fairness, and steadiness, guiding members along a process that puts a high value on the relationships in the group and also maximizes the creative possibilities of resolving the substantive issues to the satisfaction of the members. That cannot always be achieved because some people's conflict styles may not allow room for the creative work or the relationships to be adequately valued. But leaders can help the group aim for that best outcome, grounded in the creative work of the Spirit and our willingness to look for solutions that meet the best interests of everyone.

To illustrate the kinds of conflict styles people tend to fall into, let's look at a graph I developed based on the conflict management theory of social psychologist Jay Hall, Ph.D.

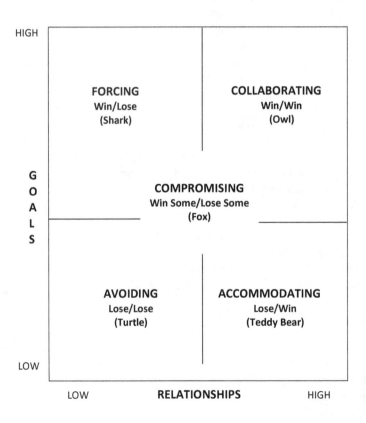

CONFLICT MANAGEMENT STYLE PREFERENCES

The graph provides four quadrants, with a fifth style in the center, formed by two scales measuring high or low interest in achieving goals and maintaining relationships. When a person has a high interest in achieving his or her goals and a high interest in maintaining the quality of the relationships with others, the style is collaborative. That style is best suited for spiritual companionship groups, where our aim is to build a strong sense of community and get peoples' needs reasonably met. When conflicts occur the collaborative style may take longer to settle the dispute because the approach seeks to build consensus around a solution where everyone gets his or her needs met. This approach is best for issues that are important to everyone and when people are willing to live prayerfully and creatively in the tension of trying to find a breakthrough idea that everyone can agree upon as an elegant solution. The next best approach for resolving substantial issues in a spiritual companionship group is a compromise style where there is give-and-take that results in the best possible outcome while preserving the integrity of the group and its relationships.

Sometimes we find people who want their goal met at all costs regardless of the relationships, the win/lose forcing style. Although less likely to happen in a spiritual companionship group, it is still possible. Such an approach should be confronted as inappropriate to the core values of the group even though it might be useful in some other situations. In other words, the person can be encouraged to change her or his approach to a style that values the group members if she or he wishes to remain in the group.

More difficult in some ways are members who use a style that either undervalues getting goals met out of a fear of hurting the relationships (accommodation), or who are just afraid of any conflict and so value neither their own goals nor the relationships (avoidance). Sometimes the issue is not that important, and so accommodation may be an acceptable stance with a quick fix. But to opt out of a dispute out of fear is a spiritual loss to the person and the group as a whole.

We are to speak our truth with love while listening to everyone else in the same spirit. Out of this honesty and humility can emerge a new creation, born of the Spirit in our midst. The leader should hold each of the members and the group as a whole to that standard.

Multicultural, Age, and Gender Diversity Considerations

Group leaders need to be aware of their own social location, recognizing their social position in the dynamics of power within a particular group and how the members will perceive their leadership authority. For example, I am white, male, heterosexual, highly educated, professional, a member of the clergy, and moving into senior status. The dominant culture gives me authority and privilege far disproportionate to many other people. How I use that authority is crucial. Leadership authority is power given in trust that it will be used for the well-being and good of the members of the group. A leader can have *power over* others or *share power with* others. If the group's members share the same social position with the leader then it is not difficult to assure that each of the members share in the power of the group equally and feel able to participate freely in the group's activities and decisions.

However, often the group's members are not in the same social locations. Women have often been taught to defer to men, while men have often been encouraged to speak up and be assertive in social situations. It is not uncommon for some women to have to struggle to find their voice in a group. Members of racial minorities may find it difficult to offer their views without first receiving permission from the leader. Asians have often been taught that it is impolite to make direct eye contact with others. People from cultures that emphasize the importance of the common good and the community may find it difficult to speak as individuals, fearing it is disrespectful to the community. Younger people may have been taught that it is disrespectful to speak unless an elder gives them permission. Differences in economic and social status may impede the free flow of deep and intimate sharing. Where Western cultures might emphasize members directly engaging each other when there are differences of opinion and disagreements, Eastern cultural approaches to managing conflict tend to be indirect and place importance on saving face. All of these present obvious challenges in leading a group.

Eric Law, a Chinese-American Episcopal priest and consultant in multicultural leadership, has developed a "mutual invitation" method of engaging in conversation that I have found to be especially helpful in the beginning stage of a small group.[3] In the mutual invitation method the leader invites a group member to speak. That member may either speak or pass or ask to speak later. However, after that person has spoken or declared his or her desire to pass or speak later, that person invites another group member to speak. That process continues until everyone has been invited to speak. Alternative ways to get everyone to speak include using a talking stick (or handheld cross or a votive candle or rock or some other object) that gives whoever holds the object the authority to speak. The talking stick then gets passed to another member or is placed in the center of the group until someone takes it and speaks. The leader should also be aware of people who are reticent to speak and invite them to share their thoughts.

Group Life Span

Every group has a life span and it is wise to think strategically about that fact. Many of the spiritual companionship group forms lend themselves to a short-term group (perhaps meeting from four to eight sessions) with the option for members to either leave after the term is over or recommit to another series of meetings. Some church-based small groups lend themselves to meeting for a season in the liturgical year. Some groups do well to start with a short series so members can test how it fits for them and then provide a long-term or ongoing group opportunity if there is sufficient interest. Long-term groups are more likely to have fewer new members join once they are well established since they have so much collective shared experience. Long-term groups also tend to die out by member attrition unless there is an alternative strategy that the group adopts. A leadership concern is when and how to bring a long-term group to an end before it dwindles in energy and sputters out after a long demise.

However, everything in the created order eventually dies and groups are no exception to this rule. Ideally a group (long- or short-term) can have a dignified ending that celebrates the meaning the group has had for its members, celebrates the depth of relationships that have been shared, and blesses the members in their leaving while supporting them in their search for new ways of being in companionship with others. I was a convener and member of a small *Contemplative Prayer* group that continued for twelve years. It went through lean times when there were few members attending and full times when everyone was present. However, when my wife (also a member) and I were about to move to another part of the country, we as a group needed to begin the process of ending the group. We discussed how we would end the group over a few of our weekly sessions and some group e-mails. Finally, we decided on a day when we would have our final session and made plans to go out for lunch together after our prayer session. Over a leisurely meal (not a practice we had ever done as part of the group) we had ample time to reflect on our group's life, to speak to each other about how important we had been to each other, and to say our goodbyes. It felt like a respectful completion of our group life.

Leadership Ethics

When we take on the role of leader for a spiritual companionship group, we are responsible for the well-being of that group and for assuring the safety of its members. We should hold ourselves to appropriate standards of leadership ethics. Ethics guidelines available through organizations such as Spiritual Directors International or spiritual direction training programs and organizations can be helpful resources.[4] I want to highlight some considerations here.

The leader is not normally considered to be in a peer relationship with other group members. The role places the leader in a position of power, and the group gives the leader implicit trust that the power will be used for the well-being of each individual in the group and of the group as a whole. The leader must assume responsibility for guiding the group in the pursuit of its purpose and tasks while maintaining a safe environment for a spiritual community to thrive. Conducting one-self in a manner that is respectful of the group's and its members' safety is a sacred imperative. Inappropriate romantic or sexual relationships, comments that can be interpreted as abusive or sexualizing the environment, or statements or actions that belittle, dominate, or offend others are betrayals of the trust and power the group gives to the leader and are ethical breaches or violations.

Whether the leader considers himself or herself as powerful in the group or not, the leader must recognize that the role creates a power imbalance. That need for recognition of the power differential and the responsibility for the right use of the power conferred upon the leader came to me most clearly years ago in a conversation we clergy had in a professional support group in the aftermath of sexual misconduct by a fellow clergyman. Although we all recognized that we carry an authority and power entrusted to us as clergy, none of us *felt* powerful. Instead, we felt we were considered marginal to our society and relatively powerless. But regardless of our self-perception, we needed to recognize that we did have power and must always conduct ourselves in a way that respected the power and authority entrusted to us by the church and society. So, too, group leaders need to be aware of the power differential and respectfully manage that power in the service of the group and its members.

The leader should avoid dual relationships where there are potential conflicts of interest if at all possible or discuss openly those possible conflicts so members are free to negotiate the implications. If the group is part of the ministry of a church community, it is likely that the leader is in other relationships with some of the members. For example, a pastor leading a small group in a church has a potential dual relationship that should be considered. Information might be shared in the group by a member or the pastor that could potentially conflict with their leadership and pastoral responsibilities with the larger church community.

A group leader should find other ways than that particular group alone to meet his or her spiritual and emotional needs. When providing leadership for a spiritual companionship group, it is well for leaders to have an active personal spiritual life and resources, such as a spiritual director and church community, to support their spiritual health. Part of that support should be outside individual or group supervision of their leadership. We will discuss this in greater detail later in this chapter when we look at a model of peer supervision and consultation for group leaders.

A Spirituality of
Group Leadership

I encourage spiritual companionship group leaders to also be participants to the degree it is possible to do both. Nevertheless, it is a different experience being a leader and facilitator of a group's process than it is being a participant member. Spiritual companionship group leadership is a ministry of service to the members, to the life of the group, the movements of the session, and to the Divine Presence active in the group. When leading a group the leader's attention is distributed beyond the scope of the participating members. It is similar to the difference between being a member of a congregation in worship and a leader of the worship. For a liturgical leader it is possible to be praying and worshipping while in the service, but it will be a different experience than the worshiper in the congregation. So, too, the leader may need to give up some freedoms to enter fully into the group's exercises to attend to the needs of the group and its members.

For example, when I lead a *Contemplative Prayer* group and we enter into the silence, I feel more like a surface diver who goes down looking for oysters with pearls but needs to come up regularly to the surface for air than a deep sea diver who has a long supply of air and can stay under the surface for an extended period of time. In the group, I frequently return from my prayer depths to see how people are doing and to check the time and monitor the felt sense of the group. So my prayer is different when I am leading. Or if I am leading a guided imagery meditation for a group, I try to enter into the meditation myself, but I am likely only to get a hazy impression of the scene and my imaginative actions. I rarely experience the clarity and level of engagement that I have when I am free to be the meditator. I let this go in service to the group because I need to be attentive to the needs of the members and the pacing of the meditation.

Leading is a responsibility but it is also a wonderful privilege. People trust us with their time and spiritual well-being, and we need to be worthy of that trust. That means we as leaders need to be prayerful before and in the midst of the group's session, and know that we depend on God's grace working with our intentions and skill. The privilege to serve people in this way also calls us to thoroughly plan and prepare in advance of the session. Because we are stewards of the sacred and servants of the group's members, our preparation and facilitation should be exemplary.

But there is another part of leadership to be appreciated: it is a joyful thing to witness how God works in these groups. So I experience both a sense of responsible servanthood and also a letting-go of the need to control a group, relaxing into a confidence that God's power and wisdom is at work in me and in the members of the group. Like the integration of the energies of Jesus' friends, Mary and Martha (see Luke 10:38–42), when I am at my best in group leadership I feel liberated to both serve my friends and enjoy the Holy One in our midst.

Training and Care of Group Leaders

There are institutions that provide formal training programs or courses in group leadership.[5] However, many churches or organizations try to do the bulk of this training by drawing on their own internal leadership resources. I recommend that at least some of the training come from professional consultants and spiritual directors who have experience with groups. Some will have formal training sessions for all new group leaders who are then commissioned to serve in their church or organization. An effective grassroots training method (in addition to formal training noted above) is to apprentice a trainee to an experienced group leader. Sometimes a group will produce its own budding leaders. The group leader should be on the lookout for those potential leaders and mentor them into their own leadership capacities. Some groups grow by cell division, and an apprentice can then take on full leadership once the group has grown enough to divide into two groups.

Case Example: Small-Group Ministry at All Souls, Berkeley

In my associate priest relationship with All Souls Episcopal Parish, Berkeley, California, I have been involved in developing a program for training, formation, and support of small-group leaders at the church. We at All Souls have a small-group steering committee (of which I am a member) that is charged with this program for the parish community. A task force was set up in 2009 in response to a vestry (the church board) invitation because the vestry had identified small groups as one of the main areas of emphasis in 2009–10. The task force in January 2010 recommended to the vestry the formation of a steering committee charged with facilitating new small-group formation and supporting new and existing small groups. The steering committee had its first meeting at the end of October 2010. A lay member of the parish chairs the committee and the rector (head pastor) is an active member.

At the first meeting the steering committee agreed to aim for launching three or four new small groups in fall 2011. A strategy for recruitment, publicity, training, and support was developed over the next several meetings. We identified the qualities we were looking for in potential small-group leaders and drew up a list of people we wished to invite to an information session on the small-group ministry. Those people were personally invited to attend the introductory meeting in February, but the meeting was also publicized, inviting anyone interested to attend.

The introductory meeting was a forty-five-minute session of talking about the parish goal of building a small-group ministry with the aim of launching some new small groups beginning in the fall, having a training program and working with potential leaders in mutual discernment about leading small groups for the parish or in other settings, and developing an ongoing support and accountability system for the parish small-group leaders. At the end of the meeting we began gathering names of those who would be interested in going through the training program.

The training program we developed initially consisted of six three-hour sessions on Sunday afternoons. This is the outline presented at the introductory meeting:

All Souls Small-Group
Leadership Training

Learning will be facilitated by a combination of presentations by the training leader and class discussions. Homework will include reading selected sections of the draft of *Where Two or Three Are Gathered* and in-class experience of core models of groups, followed by reflection on the model and observed dynamics.

Participants completing this introductory course of training will:
- understand basic dynamics of spiritual companionship-type groups
- be able to identify what models they would be most interested in leading
- be aware of the skill-set necessary to be an effective group leader
- have a deepened appreciation for the role of small groups in the life of the church
- have greater clarity about discerning a call to this ministry of group leadership

Approximate time frame for a class session:
- One hour: presentation and discussion of topics and reading
- One and a half hours: introduction of the group model to be practiced, followed by small-group practice (fishbowl with observers if necessary)
- Final half-hour: reflection on the model and dynamics

Key topics for training will include:
- creating Christian community through small groups in the church
- leadership style and behavior
- potential group member characteristics
- starting small groups
- foundation and basic structure of a spiritual companionship group
- leading group sharing
- building a supportive climate
- facilitating member participation
- group consciousness and dynamics
- handling difficulties
- group decision-making and discernment
- forming and using discussion questions
- leading group prayer
- group life span, reviews, renewal, closure
- ongoing support for leaders

Core groups practiced:
- *Circle of the Spirit* (spirituality group with led spiritual exercises and practices)
- *Holy Reading* (*lectio divina* and meditation formats for entering into the Word)
- *Contemplative Prayer* (practicing communal silent prayer and reflection)
- *Themed or Covenant Group* (such as a group that reflects on the previous Sunday's Scripture and sermon, or a covenant group such as *Benedictine Community*)
- *Group Spiritual Direction* (simple format for mutual guidance and discernment)
- *Peer Supervision and Consultation Group* (for group leaders)

Members of the steering committee participated in the training sessions alongside the seven who were being trained as small-group leaders. Having steering committee members participate as much as they were able allowed for their own formation in the All Souls style of small-group leadership and gave them important familiarity and experience for their role in the mutual discernment of the trainees.

One of the things we learned as a steering committee was how important it is to be both flexible and considerate of the training participants with this new program. We needed to come to a common understanding of what our role was in determining who would be commissioned for this ministry in the parish. Did it include discussing with each trainee our sense of their gifts and growing edges? Might someone need to be redirected because we could not affirm small-group leadership ability? Were there some criteria we could agree on for how we would decide suitability of candidates for this leadership role?

As the course neared its end, we realized that a crucial piece was missing. In the six sessions, I led all the small-group practice models (introducing a new model each session). In so doing, we had not allowed the trainees the formation experience of leading a practice session. The trainees needed the opportunity to develop and lead a group session and then reflect on their leadership experience and receive feedback from the group members. So we added that as an addition to the six core training sessions. After each trainee led a session (we divided into two small-group teams, each composed of trainees and committee members), we were better able to discern leadership gifts.

At All Souls we expect our leaders to offer their small groups in the fall and run for a term, after which members in the group will be free to leave or continue. The group may add new members, end the group, or offer a new focus. Winter term may provide other new groups. The steering committee will have periodic training sessions for new leaders. All small-group leaders are expected to meet regularly for peer supervision and consultation, and the steering committee is planning to meet quarterly with small-group leaders in joint sessions. We are still testing our program and making revisions as necessary.

Plans for the launch of the parish's small-group ministry included a commissioning of the small-group leaders and the steering committee at the main service of Eucharist on a Sunday. Several group leaders gave brief statements about their small groups at announcement time on Sundays during the sign-up period.

We established our fall small-group offerings and published them with sign-up requests (maximum of 6–7 participants for each small group). One group was co-led while the others were led by a single leader. The initial offerings provided two groups using a modification of the *Holy Reading* model, one using the *Benedictine Community* model, one group entitled "Music for the Soul" that was an experiment in *musica divina* (adapting *lectio divina* to music), and one group applied the *Companions in Transition* model. One of the *Holy Reading* groups was undersubscribed and cancelled. But four groups met through the fall term. All of the groups met at church.

All of the groups that ran during the fall term of 2011 are planning on continuing in the winter/spring term that will run from February through May 2012. Some members of the groups will be leaving and the groups will be opened to receive new members. Two additional groups will be offered for that term as a result of the steering committee conducting an intensive training for several people who already have small-group leadership experience. Both of those new groups will be co-led.

Group leaders are expected to serve in that capacity for a minimum of one year, with the opportunity to renew their commitment at the end of each year. The steering committee will provide training for additional small-group leaders on a periodic basis, as well as support current small-group leaders and monitor the program.

Ongoing Support

Ongoing support of group leaders is an important part of their care. My hope is that group leaders have sources of support beyond the group that they lead. A spiritual director, a spiritual direction peer supervision group, and/or a separate group in which the person is a member can help provide that valuable support. The following is a model of a *Leaders Group* that gives important support and growth to spiritual companionship group leaders. I have used this form of *Leaders Group* in various training programs, and it is now being used at All Souls for its small-group leaders.

Model 11:
Leaders Group

Focus
The *Leaders Group* provides peer supervision and consultation for leaders of spiritual companionship groups.

Background
It can be helpful for group leaders to have others to support them in the work of small-group and retreat development and facilitation. You may recall that in the eighteenth century, Methodists developed a small-group system of classes, bands, and select bands. The select band was a group designed to support the leaders of the classes and bands. Currently in the structure of megachurches that see themselves as a church

of small groups, there is a similar design where all small-group leaders are themselves in small groups to support them in their spiritual lives and provide a place to reflect on the processes of their group and other leadership issues. This can be a great help to group leaders, whether such a group is exclusive to small-group leaders within the organization or outside a particular organization and open to small-group and retreat leaders in the region.

Group Form

The group that I am proposing has been used in my training of group and retreat leaders through Lamb & Lion Spiritual Guidance Ministries, an Advanced Spiritual Group Leadership seminary course, and through the Group Spiritual Companionship program at the Institute of Spiritual Companionship. It is also the model that we are using at All Souls Parish in Berkeley for their small-group leaders. The format, a simple adaptation of the model that the Shalem Institute developed, has been widely used for many years for peer supervision of spiritual directors. Additionally, many spiritual directors who also lead groups or retreats use their peer supervision group for reflection on their group practice.

The primary purpose of the group is mutually to support group leaders in their spiritual lives as they engage in the practice of leading spiritual companionship groups. The supervision dimension of the group provides the opportunity for a leader-presenter to explore what is going on within himself/herself in a group situation from the presenter's practice. Reflection on the inner psycho-spiritual dynamics of the presenter provides accountability for his or her development as a group leader. Questions that the peer-group members ask are intended to assist the presenter in exploring her or his spiritual reality rather than problem-solving or managing the group.

I call this a peer supervision *and* consultation group because with small groups there is another layer of planning, development, and relational dynamics with the broader organization (if attached to an organization), and complicated group dynamics involved in group or retreat leadership, in addition to the usual concerns of supervision groups for spiritual directors. So there is a greater need for peer consultation when doing this group work. For example, let's say I have been in conversation with a local church's pastor and have agreed to lead a parish retreat on the topic of spirituality and social action. I discover that as I am preparing for this retreat I am growing anxious about my ability to lead adequately on this topic. I am personally committed to social action and spirituality but I am not sure how to frame this in a retreat form that supports retreatants' efforts at integrating spirituality and action. The *Leaders Group* can help me explore my anxious feelings and how I hold that in my spiritual life (supervision), and also may give me the opportunity to explore some ideas and receive feedback out of their experience about how I might frame the retreat (consultation).

Leaders' Peer Supervision
and Consultation Group Process

The group decides the process of determining who will be the presenter(s). Either a presenter(s) can be assigned prior to the meeting or this can spontaneously arise from the check-in time with a person(s) saying they would like some focus time. If the presenter is pre-scheduled, is there openness to providing some focused time from others if they ask for it at check-in?

1. Opening spiritual exercise or prayer led by facilitator.

2. Check-in (both about personal life and group/retreat work) initiated by facilitator.

3. Facilitator calls for silent centering time (about 2–5 minutes) until the presenter is ready to speak.

4. Presenter(s) describes a situation related to group/retreat work.

5. Facilitator asks the group if there are any questions of clarification.

6. Facilitator calls the group to a period of silent prayer (about 3–5 minutes) to center everyone.

7. Peer group assists the presenter in exploring the issues (especially the inner experience) related to the situation.

8. Facilitator calls for the group to hold the presenter in prayer silently or spoken (1–2 minutes).

9. Discussion of related issues and experiences that the presentation evoked for others or other questions and concerns related to group/retreat ministry if time permits.

10. Process review of this meeting (what went well and what might be improved) and/or suggestions for modifying future meetings. Other items for the group's maintenance?

11. Closing prayer led by facilitator.

This model should be open to adaptation depending on the needs of the group. For example, if the *Leaders Group* is also entrusted with leadership within the organization (such as being the small-groups steering committee for a church), then discussions and decisions related to the organization may need to be done either at a separate meeting or incorporated into the structure of this session. However, since the primary purpose of this group is to provide spiritual support and leadership development for its members, this purpose should not be eclipsed by organizational demands.

It is not unusual in peer supervision/consultation that the issues a presenter brings up for reflection also may evoke related issues or topics of interest for others in the group. Having a step in the session (number 9 above) to explore such topics or issues among group members, within the time parameters, can be a rich element of professional group support.

Resources

Henry Cloud and John Townsend, *Making Small Groups Work.* I have used this book as a training text and have received mixed reviews, along with my personal ambivalence. The language is clearly coming from an evangelical perspective and needs reinterpretation for those who do not share that view. But there is much that is helpful in the book. It is a well-organized and thorough primer for small-group leaders and provokes thought about many situations in small-group dynamics. The perspective is compassionate, psychologically informed, and assumes that the small group is a powerful medium for spiritual and emotional growth.

Bill Donahue, *Leading Life-Changing Small Groups.* Donahue is the spokesman for the megachurch approach to small groups. This book is a user-friendly training manual in small groups from the evangelical Willow Creek experience. Many kinds of small groups (hundreds) make up the building blocks of the church.

Edwin H. Friedman, *Generation to Generation: Family Process in Church and Synagogue.* The primary text on family-systems theory.

Thomas G. Kirkpatrick, *Small Groups in the Church: A Handbook for Creating Community.* An alternative to Donahue's work, this book is from a mainstream church perspective and shows how a small-group ministry can be incorporated into a church's structure. In this resource, small groups are seen as supporting the whole church's mission and ministry.

M. Scott Peck, M.D., *The Different Drum: Community Making and Peace.* This is my primary choice in required reading on group dynamics. It is not without limitations—particularly Peck's irritating (to me) claim to have achieved community in x number of minutes. In addition, the political examples later in his book are dated to the Reagan presidential era. But the late Scott Peck's work on community-making is heartfelt as well as informed.

We have covered a lot of territory in this chapter, and this is merely a beginning to considerations about issues of small-group dynamics and leadership. But having a beginner's mind (as our Buddhist friends say) is appropriate in all this. Christians might suggest that the virtue of humility is or should be well practiced in this ministry of small-group leadership.

chapter eight

Special Applications

JUST AS SPIRITUAL direction attributes (such as respect for silence, cultivating a capacity for holy listening, and having a contemplative stance) can be applied to many situations outside a formal spiritual direction relationship, many of the attributes and models of spiritual companionship can be translated into settings and situations other than a typical ninety-minute small-group gathering. In this chapter we will explore some of those applications.

Retreat Leadership

Let's take a look at some retreat forms with an eye to group spiritual leadership. One form of retreat is a personal silent retreat that an individual might take at a retreat center or hermitage setting. This could take the form of an undirected retreat, or the person might ask for a meeting or series of meetings with a spiritual director during the retreat.

A church, group, or organization might make arrangements for a directed silent retreat or a contemplative retreat. Again, this is structured around allowing time for silence with some common prayer, along with a spiritual director available for personal meetings with retreatants. Jane Vennard's book *Be Still: Designing and Leading Contemplative Retreats* is a useful resource for planning this and the next type of retreat.

A church, group, or organization might also arrange with a leader to provide a facilitated group retreat or day of reflection. This might be a one-day retreat, or held over multiple days. In this situation a leader plans the retreat with the particular group or organization. There is likely to be a specific theme and goals for the group. For example, I worked with a counseling center to lead them in one of their annual one-day retreats. The center had been through a time of change and stress, and in consultation with their executive director I offered a retreat that provided what I called "integrative spiritual practices" for them to experience together and share. The exercises were similar to those I would draw upon in a *Circle of the Spirit* group. Here is the outline we followed:

Gathered in Wholeness:
Integrative Spiritual Practices

1. Check-in (10 minutes)

2. Introduction to Gathered in Wholeness Retreat (20 minutes)
    Integrative Spiritual Practices
    (*Gather Us, O God*—Monica Brown chant)
    Invitation throughout day: creating your mandala

3. Short Break (5 minutes)

4. Body (90 minutes)
    Qi Gong—Eight Pieces of Silk—with meditation questions
    (*Inside Chants*—background music)
    Lunch includes possible mandala work (60 minutes)

5. Spirit and Soul (85 minutes)
    Spirit/Soul Timeline—includes mandala work and break (45 minutes)
    (*Flute Dreams* and *Officium*—background music)
    Sharing in group (40 minutes)

6. Short Break (5 minutes)

7. Mind: (45 minutes)
    Lectio Divina—individual or group options
    (Chime)

8. Break and mandala work (15 minutes)

9. Honoring the Dimensions (30 minutes)
    (Tibetan Singing Bowl)
    Showing mandalas
    (*Gather Us, O God*—Monica Brown chant)

10. Four Elements Meditation

11. Evaluation

Groups for which I have led retreats or reflection days have included church boards, individual churches or a partnership of churches, clergy groups, men's and women's groups, a yoga center, a school for deacons, a pastoral counseling center, a group leadership formation program, seminary retreats for entering or graduating students, and church staff. I have often drawn on the *Circle of the Spirit* format for use in these retreats, along with *Holy Reading* group resources and sometimes *Dreamwork* resources. Topics have included exploring practices for wholeness, discernment practices for individuals or groups, ways of praying and meditating, men's/women's spirituality, healing the wounds of a community, dreamwork for inner wisdom, exploring spiritual paths, ways of engaging Scripture, spirituality of leadership, and more.

My friend and Group Spiritual Leadership graduate John Lionberger provides guided interfaith group retreats in the wilderness through his Renewal in the Wilderness ministry.[1] His book, by the same name, gives wonderful descriptions of themes and experiences from these retreats, including his own fascinating initial encounter with the Divine on a stark, frozen lake in the Minnesota Boundary Waters that became the seed of his spiritual awakening and eventual ministry.

A variation on the facilitated multiple-day group retreat is the Retreat in the Midst of Life. I have team-led or served as a spiritual director for this form of retreat through a seminary and a church. This retreat is popular with Roman Catholic churches. It is a practical alternative to trying to get a group away on a multiple-day retreat, because the parish or organization hosts the limited meetings and the rest of the retreat is done by the retreatants in about a half-hour's time daily in their own setting and at their own convenience. In this format a theme is introduced, and there might be a short opening and closing event scheduled at the host site. Retreatants are given a packet of materials that could be helpful for them to use on their own time over the period of days the retreat is scheduled, and some particular times are scheduled for participants if they wish to meet with a spiritual guide (and if it is part of the church tradition to make a sacramental confession with a priest) at the host site. The packet of materials might include *Circle of the Spirit*-type exercises or *lectio divina* opportunities with suggested Scripture passages.

Here is an example of how a team of us at Seabury-Western Theological Seminary presented a Retreat in the Midst of Life in October 2003:

Listening for the Voice of the Beloved:
A Retreat in the Midst of Life

What is a retreat in the midst of life?

Often it is not feasible to stop everything and go on retreat, but it is possible to integrate some focused periods of meditation into one's life for a designated period of days. After several weeks of immersion in the seminary term, it is easy to lose sight of why we are here and Whose we are.

Plan to participate in this Retreat in the Midst of Life.

Allow yourself time to listen for the voice of the One who loves you.

Participation recommendations:

◆ Engage in one meditation each day (Tuesday, Wednesday, Thursday) at a time of your own choosing.

◆ Examine the packet offering a range of possible meditation materials (including selections from Scripture, instructions for a guided imagery mediation, a walking meditation, an icon for contemplation, etc.).

◆ Meet with a spiritual guide for a thirty-minute consultation once during the retreat period.

◆ Sign up several days before the retreat begins for appointment times to meet with spiritual guides during the retreat period.

◆ Reflect on your retreat experience with the help of spiritual guides.

◆ Participate in the sacrament of reconciliation offered by Episcopal priest guides if you desire.

As the seminary chaplain I contracted with some spiritual directors and priests in the area to be available at different times of the day and evening for the thirty-minute sessions and arranged rooms for them to see retreatants. People interested in meeting for a consultation signed up for a time with the guide of their choosing.

Organizational Spiritual Guidance

There are different ways that skills and forms for leading spiritual companionship groups might be applied to organizational-level spiritual guidance. I have already discussed retreat or quiet day/day of reflection leadership. Sometimes organizations need an outside consultant to assist with helping frame and facilitate conversation about institutional concerns.

For example, a not-for-profit, faith-based residential senior center asked me about facilitating a conversation between staff and residents. After I had a preliminary meeting with the staff, we set up a productive conversation among all parties. Here is the outline I used:

Exploring Our Life Together

1. Gathering and Settling In (10 minutes)

2. Welcome and Description of the Morning (20 minutes)
    What will help us speak openly and respectfully to each other this morning? (put on newsprint)
    Ask for commitment to "try it on" for the morning
    Separate groups of residents, students, staff at four tables of five to seven people
    Have table groups discuss and a table member report to everyone

3. Focus on Our Senior Residents (30 minutes)
    - things we appreciate about (about being) residents at this house
    - concerns we have about (as) residents
    - questions we have for our residents, with opportunity for responses
    - things we want everyone to understand about us as residents

4. Short Break (5 minutes)

5. Focus on Our Student Helpers (30 minutes)
    - things we appreciate about (about being) student helpers
    - concerns we have about (as) student helpers
    - questions we have for our student helpers, with opportunity for responses
    - things we want everyone to understand about us as student helpers

6. Break (10 minutes)

7. Focus on Our Staff (30 minutes)
    * things we appreciate about (about being) staff
    * concerns we have about (as) staff
    * questions we have for our staff
    * things we want everyone to understand about us as staff

8. Stretch Break (1 minute)

9. Focus on Communication Issues (20 minutes)
    * What are things we can do to clarify misunderstandings and improve communication?
    * What are positive things we can do that would help us discuss and resolve difficult situations when they arise?

10. Movement Break (1 minute)

11. Picturing Our House (20 minutes)
    Move to larger table groups of about ten each, blending residents, students, and staff
    Have each table group draw a picture representing what the spirit of the house looks like at its best
    Present the pictures to all, with comments the group wishes to make

12. Closing Circle (5 minutes)
    In a closing circle invite people to name a word, feeling, or image that comes to them about what they are taking with them from the morning

In a time when they were under stress due to losses of members, several small churches invited me to help members work on improving communication and to guide them in looking at options for the church's future. This organizational consulting had many qualities of group spiritual companionship leadership connected with it. Coaching people into deep, respectful listening, using imaginative processes for exploring issues facing them, and seeking God's guidance in the midst of difficult situations are all dimensions of group spiritual guidance.

Many of these spiritual guidance skills have been called into use in my roles as the chaplain for a seminary, the rector at a church, a consultant, and a support priest working with churches in the midst of transitions. Another spiritual director, a Presbyterian, was invited to be a spiritual companion for an Episcopal church undergoing a change in leadership. He could bring the gift of being an unattached, caring, nonanxious, faithful, listening presence to an organization that was going through a time of transition.

As a consultant and organizational spiritual guide, I have used communal dreamwork methods for church leaders, a parachurch organization, and in discernment to consider the possibility of setting up a spirituality center in Chicago. Whenever I have asked a group of people if anyone has had a dream that they feel is related to their organization, someone has always shared a dream. The resulting dreamwork has raised significant issues for the organization and provided a non-threatening way to begin discussing them.

Interfaith and Secular Groups

It is my contention that there is nowhere God is not. Given that orientation, spiritual companionship groups in various adapted forms can be supportive for people in interfaith settings as well as secular contexts. Dreaming, for example, is a universal human experience, and so a *Dreamwork* group supporting each member in exploring the multiple possible meanings of his or her dreams is a good choice for interfaith or secular settings. An online *Dreamwork* group that I facilitate incorporates pagan as well as Christian perspectives while recognizing the vast areas of commonality in a rich experience of shared reflections on possible meaning.

Modifications of the *Holy Reading* group model, for example by using poetry, especially from Middle Eastern mystical poets like Hafiz, Rumi, or Kabir, as well as Western poets, could enrich meditation and *lectio divina* practices. Like dreamwork, engaging poetry, visual art, chant and circle dance, or meditative movement can be less threatening to interfaith groups. I have appreciated the work of Brother Joseph Kilikevice at the Shem Center for Interfaith Spirituality[2] in the Chicago area and in his retreats. His work includes creating Circles of Respect, a masterful ritual use of Dances of Universal Peace,[3] and meditations drawing on the wisdom of many faith traditions.

Two participants in the Group Spiritual Companionship program were interested in providing support groups for healthcare providers. Janice Zeller and Anne McGovern offered a well-attended workshop for those involved in healthcare professions at the pre-conference for the Spiritual Directors International's 2009 gathering. Dr. Zeller offers "Circles of Care"—ongoing, supportive healing groups in a healthcare setting. She writes that she has "been asked to adapt this group spiritual direction model for use with older adults who are experiencing transitional life events and/or are seeking meaning in life." Her classmate Anne McGovern also made a proposal to bring "Circles of Renewal" groups to healthcare professionals and following training was pursing pilot programs at two hospitals.[4]

Sensitivity to how spiritual or religious language may affect people in interfaith or secular settings is among the most important concerns. Zeller and McGovern drew from the basic *Circle of the Spirit* model, but found that changing the group name to "Circles of Care" and "Circles of Renewal" may make it more accessible to a wider field of people. Some people, to be sure, would be comfortable with language that speaks of God or Spirit, but for others it may get in the way. Also, a secular organization may have policies around what programs can and cannot be offered.

When I asked some of my former seminary students what they were doing in small groups, one of the most moving reflections I heard was from the Reverend Cliff Haggenjos, who was ministering near San Quentin Prison. Cliff wrote that he has been a member of the Kairos prison ministry and through Kairos he met someone who invited him to be part of the Monday Night Centering Prayer Group at San Quentin Prison. His experience of being part of this team that meets with ten to fifteen prisoners has been profound for him.

> We practice Centering Prayer in the following fashion: a 30-minute prayer session, followed by a "prayer walk" around the chapel, followed by another 30-minute prayer session. After a 10–15 minute break, we then finish with a period of *lectio divina* and sharing. Each of us takes turns leading the group, and we also spend time in one-on-one discussion with the men. ... It is hard to describe how powerful the Presence can feel at times in this group. Many of the men in the group have committed some horrific crimes, but through their time in prison have come to find the love of Our Lord, and the sense of spiritual wholeness that I get from them is amazing. ... As you are aware, when we are engaged in Centering Prayer, the group becomes quite silent. The stillness of the chapel is something I have come to appreciate, especially after talking with the men. They describe to me how special the group is to them because of this quiet stillness. As you might imagine, life inside the prison walls is a terribly noisy, terribly loud experience. The men relate how you have to get used to sleeping with ear plugs, because it is often the only way to shut the noise out—it remains throughout the evening as well as through the day. So for these men, the two hours they spend on Monday night in the chapel—sitting in silence—well, those minutes become a huge blessing for all of the men. As for me, hearing of their experiences, I have come to value that silence, and its amazing sacredness, all the more.[5]

Diane Millis, Ph.D., is director of the Journey Conversations Project that provides small-group processes that may involve interfaith conversations. She outlined these steps for interfaith group spiritual companioning based on their project:

Interfaith Spiritual Companioning
through Journey Conversations

In a journey conversation, **four or more persons** gather together for **an extended conversation or a series of conversations.** Participants begin by turning off their electronic devices, slowing down and getting quiet in order to **pay attention and listen**...

Within—to their hearts and deepest truths;

to their lives—to their stories and what gives their lives meaning;

and **to one another**—to what they can discover and learn in community.

Regardless of group size or duration of meeting time, each journey conversation consists of the following contemplative practices:

Centering Practices: Contemplative practices such as shared silence, stillness, and centering on the breath prepare participants for conversation and help them maintain or regain attentive presence throughout their time together.

Sacred Reading: Participants listen deeply to wisdom literature including scriptures from the great spiritual traditions, as well as contemporary prose and poetry. Listening to wisdom born from the lived experience of people and communities who are seeking truth prepares participants to notice and welcome the wisdom that lives in each member of the group.

Storytelling: During each gathering, one or more participants share their stories in response to the guiding questions tailored to the conversational context and aims, e.g.,:

1. What have been the key events on your journey?
2. Which persons have had the most significant influence on your faith journey? What have they taught you?
3. Who is God for you, or what is your understanding of the Sacred, at this time in your life? How has your understanding of God changed over the course of your journey? What images of God are most meaningful for you?

4. What are the places that are sacred for you?

5. What activities increase your awareness of the presence of God/Spirit?

6. What are some of your favorite hymns, passages from sacred texts or inspirational quotes that have sustained you on your journey?

Compassionate Listening: As others tell their stories, participants are invited to suspend their self-oriented, reactive thinking and open their awareness to notice what is going on within themselves as they listen to others speak.

Compassionate Responding: Following each person's story, participants respond by offering the gift of questions. These questions are intended to be compassionate and evocative, inviting the storyteller to reflect more deeply on his or her experience.

Collective Reflection: Conversations conclude with some time for quiet to honor what has been shared and to invite participants to briefly describe what they have discovered and learned.[6]

Internet Virtual Groups

There has been a long tradition of corresponding by letter between spiritual friends or with a spiritual director. With the advent of e-mail, Internet message board services, virtual environments, and audio and visual conferencing, the capacity to bridge space between people instantaneously (synchronous sessions) or at the convenience of members (asynchronous sessions) provides new opportunities for group spiritual companionship. Do a computer search for "groups" and see how many listings you get.

At the time of this writing I am teaching two completely online continuing education courses for the Church Divinity School of the Pacific's Center for Anglican Learning and Leadership, both related to spiritual direction and group spiritual companionship. I offer a telephone conference call with my students (where we are all connected at the same time), and the rest of the course is done using a forum/message board platform. We see a photo of each other. We write to each other in week-long units when it is convenient. Students get lectures and other course information from the learning website. The Internet connects us across two countries.

I also coordinate a *Leaders Group* for virtual peer supervision and consultation that uses a message board platform. We are experimenting with how we want to structure our meetings, but currently we are working with this process:

Process Guide for a Monthly
Virtual Group Session

Days 1–2: *Facilitator opens the session and group members check in*
The facilitator opens the meeting on the first of the month and invites everyone to check in with what they want the group to know about their current personal life and group leadership situation.

Day 3: *Presenter brings group a situation to explore*
The presenter shares a situation from some group experience (does not have to be a situation where the presenter is the leader) to explore some issue, question, dynamics, impact of their spiritual life, etc. Group members ask questions for clarification of the presentation.

Days 4–5: *Group responds to presenter*
Group members respond to the presenter, offering evocative questions, images, experiences, support, etc. More emphasis is on helping the presenter explore his or her own understanding as a group leader and how the situation affects his or her own spiritual life than on consulting and providing how-to answers.

Days 6–7: *Hear final thoughts from group, hold a process review, and close the session*
Group members share any reflections and responses about issues that came up for them from the exploration with the presenter. Then facilitator checks with members on how we did on the process, clarifies who is scheduled for next month's facilitator and presenter, and closes the meeting.

Remainder of month: *Open to general conversations*
Members are free to invite other discussion, and share in other ways related to our group's sense of community. If some members were away for portions of the session, this could be an opportunity to add their voices. This is our "parking lot discussions" between sessions.

Another ongoing group that I started in November 2010 after beta-testing it earlier in the year is the online *Dreamwork* group. Since the onset, the ongoing group has had a pagan member along with others who are Christian. This group has a six-day extended session for asynchronous messages. I move the group through its process steps over the week. Then we take a week off before starting another session. At the end of eight sessions members can elect to continue or leave the group. Continuing members can negotiate the frequency of meetings and invite new members to join. The following is a guide to the *Dreamwork* group's process in the online session that runs over the course of about a week. The italicized portions give general time frames on the steps of the extended session:

Online Dreamwork Group
Process Guide

[In advance of the first session, ask for a volunteer willing to share a dream for the step 3 focused dream sharing.]

Monday morning (or Sunday night) send members a posting for steps 1–3. In that posting introduce yourself and share one of your dreams. Ask that all do step 2 (check-in) and step 3 (share a dream), except for the dreamer, before Tuesday.

1. Open the Session
   Facilitator begins with a simple reading, prayer, poem, or other offering.

2. Check-in
   Everyone is invited to share briefly what they wish the group to know about them at this time. The group simply receives these statements with respect as if they are a graced holding container for each other. We refrain from the urge to fix, rescue, or give advice. Just hold people lovingly in their reality.

3. General Dream Sharing
   Everyone except the member presenting a dream for focused work is invited to share a dream (old or new) or a fragment of a dream without interpretive comments. This starts to build the group's collective dream resources.

Tuesday morning (or Monday night), after everyone has completed their initial check-in and general dream sharing, ask the dreamer to share the dream we will all work on in step 4. The dreamer then shares her or his dream sometime Tuesday.

4. Focused Dreamwork
   The dreamer presents his or her dream in as much detail as possible for exploration with the group's assistance. Each session one member (or possibly two members) provides a dream for focused work, rotating the role of dreamer over the course of the series of sessions.

After the dream is shared on Tuesday we ask the dreamer questions of clarification (step 5). The dreamer responds to those questions as she or he wishes. Dedicate as much of Tuesday and Wednesday as is needed for clarifications of the dream.

5. Clarifications
   The group asks the dreamer questions to understand the dream's context and clarify details of the dream content.

When clarifications are finished, ask the group to move to step 6 and explore meaning. This movement likely occurs sometime Wednesday. The group has some of Wednesday and all of Thursday to interact with the dreamer and each other on possible meanings.

6. Explore Meaning
   Now the group engages the dreamer and each other in sharing possible meanings of dream symbols and the dream as a whole. The group may ask the dreamer what meaning the dream has at this time, or what parts of the dream the dreamer has energy around, or what the dreamer associates with particular symbols. Members may share what they associate with particular symbols and what meaning the dream holds for them. Often it is helpful to use language such as, "If this were my dream then [this symbol] would mean [this] to me." The group should first be attentive to helping the dreamer explore the dreamer's meanings. But the group should also be alert to shared social levels of meaning.

For Friday, invite all to share what they have gained from working with the dream and dreamer in step 7.

7. Facilitator Asks for Summary Statements
   The facilitator tests whether the dreamer and group feel they have sufficiently explored the dream and what new insights have emerged. Then the dreamer and all members are invited to make any summary statements on what they are taking with them from the exploration.

For Saturday, invite a review of the process (step 8) and ask for a volunteer dreamer for next Monday's session.

8. Process Review
   The facilitator asks if anyone has questions or comments about the way the group is running. Are any modifications to future sessions needed or desired? Who will be the next session's dreamer/ presenter?

Close the session by Saturday evening (step 9).

9. Closing the Session
   The facilitator shares a prayer or other simple way of ending the session.

10. Parking Lot Discussions
    As some conversation might continue following a real-time session, there might be some additional thoughts that members might want to share after the close of this session and in the days before the next session begins.

As with any small-group model, there are both advantages and limitations to using online *Dreamwork* groups:

Advantages

1. We can draw from interested people across the world.

2. The group does not have time/space restrictions.

3. Members can share after thoughtful reflection instead of having to respond immediately.

4. Members can share at times most convenient to them.

5. We are attentive to members daily over a longer period of time than in a concentrated ninety-minute session.

6. People who are physically or circumstantially restricted are free to be full participants.

7. We build a different kind of community together—a virtual network community.

8. Cost for a professionally facilitated group is likely to be comparable to or less than real-time sessions.

9. It is easier to find an experienced spiritual guidance-focused facilitator skilled at group dreamwork when not limited to those in the local area.

Limitations

1. The conversation is less spontaneous.

2. We cannot see visual cues from others about how they receive or send a communication.

3. We cannot set aside one concentrated period of time in the week to complete the meeting.

4. We will not have a real-time, real-place embodied community.

In both the online *Dreamwork* group and in the *Leaders Group* experience of an extended session, we discovered that the quality of responses was different than in real-time groups. The extended virtual session, when done asynchronously (not everyone communicating at the same time like in a real-time, ninety-minute session where everyone is gathered together), offered time to contemplate what members write and an opportunity to make reflective responses. This also is the case with personal spiritual direction by correspondence.

Leading virtual groups requires flexibility and patience. Often members will need to complete several sessions before they are fully oriented to the rhythm of extended sessions. Some people will need extra help getting set up or learning how to use online resources. Sometimes a member will be confused about when to contribute in each movement in the extended session. As a leader you may need to initiate a phone or e-mail conversation outside the group's website to check in or provide some coaching with a member who may need some help. Think of this as a hallway conversation at break time in a real-time session. For all its limitations, for some people the virtual group will have important benefits. And living in a time when social networking technologies are growing at a rapid pace, we can anticipate having increasing opportunities and requests to provide this way of spiritual companionship.

Other Long-Distance Groups

Other long-distance possibilities are opening up for real-time group interactions. Videoconferencing and teleconferencing provide the ability to be connected with others in synchronous group sessions. As previously mentioned, sometimes I use this capability to supplement the asynchronous sessions of a virtual Internet group, but this could be the primary meeting mode for a long-distance group. The tricky part is to arrive at a meeting schedule that fits everyone over different time zones.

Higher education is developing hybrid learning opportunities where courses are taught using a combination of conferencing or message-board modes along with intensive real-time face-to-face gatherings of the community in one location. This model can be adapted for long-distance groups that occasionally gather at a retreat center or other location to deepen the community relationships further.

Gathered in the
Name of the Divine

Where two or three are gathered in my name,
I am there among them.
—*Matthew 18:20*

IN THE EIGHTEENTH chapter of Matthew's gospel there is a collection of teachings attributed to Jesus, including the verse cited above
about his presence in the midst of the gathering. The paragraph to
which the saying belongs addresses issues of sins against the community and steps toward reconciliation, and concludes with an emphasis
on the spiritual authority of Jesus in union with his heavenly Father
and with those who are in his earthly community. This passage has
been taken as a promise to future generations of followers that the
Spirit of Jesus Christ is in the midst of those gathered in his name, not
just for the disciples gathered in the time of Jesus of Nazareth. This is
a powerful promise.

So, too, in spiritual companionship groups when we gather with
the intention of inviting the presence of the Holy One into our midst,
we are not alone. Our group does not simply constitute the sum of our
individual members. There is also Wisdom in our group that goes beyond us all but is available to be our guide. Christians will call upon
the divine name of Jesus Christ and ask for the Spirit of Christ's wisdom
and guidance, that we might share in the mind of Christ.[1]

Those of other faith traditions will use other names for this one in
whom we all "live and move and have our being" and who is a presence (sometimes hidden, sometimes revealed) in the midst of our group

(see Acts 17:28). John Mabry tells a delightful and saucy Hindu Rasa Dance story of girls who were cow herders and who danced one night with Krishna, who vanishes from their sight while they are dancing in a forest and then reappears as they chant his praises. Krishna says to the girls, "Sometimes I hide from you, but do not think I was away from you. I was very near and watching you."[2]

In our spiritual companionship groups we can discover that we are being transformed by the hidden Presence working in our midst. There is an apocryphal tale that has circulated widely over the years. I have seen a Jewish variant on the tale but usually it concerns a Christian monastery. Here's my own version of this tale.

One of You Is the Messiah

There was a monastery that had been going through tough times, and the numbers of monks had dwindled to only a handful. It was questionable whether the community would survive. Struggling with the challenge of leading his community in this demoralizing circumstance, the abbot paid a visit to a rabbi friend of his and poured out his heart to him. The rabbi took the matter into prayer and finally counseled his friend the abbot. "In my prayer I kept getting the sense that one of you is the Messiah. I'm not sure what it means, but it is all I can say."

The abbot was amazed and unsettled by the direction of his friend's counsel, but he took it to his community: "One of us is the Messiah."

Everyone took the words incredulously. Could it be Brother Andrew? Surely not. Not with his quarrelsome tendencies. How about Brother Patrick? The way he hoards things? Be serious. Could it be me? Oh, I know that it can't be me. And the question, followed by the negative reaction, continued around the community. But then things began to change. The monks began to ask themselves, what if it is true, what if the Messiah is here? *If* someone in the community *is* the Messiah, maybe I just don't have the skill to recognize him. Or maybe he chooses to hide his identity. Perhaps I had better listen to everyone and treat everyone *as if each* could be the one.

And so it happened that the community began to change. It became more energized. The worship was livelier, since the Messiah was there. The preaching found new depth because of the presence of the Lord. The relationships of the brothers to each other began to be more respectful and at the same time more joyful. They joined in decisions with more creative energy and with firmer confidence that God was hearing their prayers.

As the community reawakened to their sense of purpose in being together, they drew more visitors from the outside world. Some of them decided to test a call to monastic community there, and some stayed to become monks in the place where the Lord was, and the monastery grew.[3]

We are likely to discover that as we seek the sacred Presence within and around us in our circle, we are slowly becoming fully human, fully alive people who are connected with God and who show God's glory.[4] That transforming effect of spiritual companionship groups is like the *perichoresis* dance of the Holy Trinity I referred to early in this book. In love and deep respect we are called into that dance with the Divine and with one another. So this dance spills out into the world of our other relationships. While we are being transformed by living our lives with greater wholeness and attention to the Wisdom in our midst, we bring our deeper and fuller selves into our interaction with those we do not know, as well as our network of families, friends, acquaintances, workplaces, social and political structures, spiritual/religious communities, and natural environments. That small circle of a spiritual companionship group touches many people over time.

This book has been written for you to take on the role of leading others into the great dance of spiritual companionship and sacred community. These small groups and forms of mutual spiritual direction provide the medium for encounters with the hidden Divine and the deeply transforming spiritual work of its members. Spiritual companionship groups are a way that the petition in the Lord's Prayer "Thy kingdom come, Thy will be done, on earth as it is in heaven" becomes actualized in our world right now. May you discover the joy and delight of leading people into the heart of God.

Spiritual Exercises for *Circle of the Spirit* Groups and Retreats

UNLESS OTHERWISE credited, I developed the following spiritual exercises. All may be useful to adapt for group settings, and some are particularly useful for group-level reflection (such as a vestry/church board retreat) rather than for individual-level reflection shared within the group.

1. God Within You in Unity

If you love me, you will keep my commandments. And I will ask the Father, and he will give you another Advocate, to be with you forever. This is the Spirit of truth, whom the world cannot receive, because it neither sees him nor knows him. You know him, because he abides with you, and he will be in you.

I will not leave you orphaned; I am coming to you. In a little while the world will no longer see me, but you will see me; because I live, you also will live. On that day you will know that I am in my Father, and you in me, and I in you. They who have my commandments and keep them are those who love me; and those who love me will be loved by my Father, and I will love them and reveal myself to them.

—John 14:15–21

1. Try to move into a reverent, quiet place within yourself. For the duration of this meditation let the concerns that might crowd in on your consciousness be held in God's care. Let the noises that occasionally break the silence simply be, without fighting them or focusing on them. If it feels right to you, close your eyes.

2. Take some full breaths in and out. With each breath, feel yourself relaxing a little more and sinking into God's protective care and love.

3. Imagine that you are taking a journey into the deepest part of your being, your soul, and with each breath you are moving closer to your truest, finest, holiest self—your sacred center where God already abides. Notice how you feel as you move toward that center.

4. It may help to imagine that you come to a closed door in a beautiful mansion. Open the door and follow a long, well-lit hallway to another door that is the entranceway to your sacred center. When you are ready, open that door and move into your sacred center. Look around this room. See what, and perhaps who, is there. Take note of any feelings you have about being at the center of your soul.

5. Imagine that you are met there, welcomed into your sacred center, by three Beings—your Christ, your Advocate the Holy Spirit, and your Creator Father or Mother. They may come to you as symbols such as light or a dove—or they might be present to you as people (male or female) that you have known that represent true goodness and sacred health for you—or they may be people you have not met in your outer world before. Let them welcome you into their midst and surround you with the love they have for one another and for you. Take note of whatever feelings you have—and respond to them in whatever way feels right and safe to you. If they have words for you, listen to what they have to say. If you have questions or things you wish to say to them, do so—and listen to their responses. If you have the image of people or other things you wish to bring to them, you are free to do so.

6. The Holy Presences within you wish to give you a special gift: it might be a word or phrase, it might be a symbol or picture or song or some other token of your time there. Receive whatever they give you and thank them, saying goodbye in whatever way seems appropriate. Know that you can return again to your sacred center where the Holy Presences abide in unity with themselves and you.

7. When you are ready, go back to the door and open it, going through to the hallway. Close the door to the center of your soul and proceed down the lighted hallway to the outer door. Go through that door. Become aware of your gentle breath bringing you to an awareness of our outer world. Whenever you are ready, open your eyes, remembering your meditational prayer on the presence of God dwelling within you in unity with you in love.

2. Representing Your Spiritual Reality

Draw a picture that conveys your present experience of reality, of God, or of your sense of spiritual truth. It can take any form: realistic, abstract, or symbolic. Insofar as possible, let the picture draw itself (perhaps letting the picture emerge using your non-dominant hand) and think about it after, not during, the drawing process.

You may journal your thoughts and feelings associated with the picture afterwards. Does this become the subject for further prayer?

Alternatives

1. If you cannot seem to get an image to work with, perhaps a phrase comes to mind, or even some thoughts about your spiritual reality. Develop reflections or prayer on the phrase or the thoughts.

2. If nothing comes in image or thought, perhaps you can sit and gently observe the qualities of that nothing. What feelings are associated with it? Is it full or rich, filled with potential or barren or empty, or do other qualities or a mixture of qualities emerge? Does a prayer emerge for you?[1]

3. Names of God Through Your Life

There are many metaphors and images for the Sacred Mystery that we call God. Scripture offers metaphors and titles such as rock, fountain, mother hen, eagle, womb, judge, king, warrior, father, Word, deliverer, redeemer, cloud, fire, ruler of the universe, Prince of Peace. Our religious tradition has offered other metaphorical names, envisioning God as mother, lover, Holy Trinity, the one who wounds, holy mystery, light, dazzling darkness, and friend. Other religions have other names for God. None of the names are completely adequate; indeed, no combination of names will be comprehensive enough to express fully the inexpressible. In this meditation we will have the opportunity to apply names to God that have arisen from our known or intuited experience of our relationship with God in the past and our present lives, and to suggest names that express our possible future relationship.

1. Try to move into a reverent, quiet place within yourself. For the duration of this meditation, let the concerns that might crowd in on your consciousness be held in God's care. Let the noises that occasionally break the silence simply be, without fighting them or focusing on them. If it feels right to you, close your eyes.

2. Take some full breaths in and out. With each breath, feel yourself relaxing a little more and sinking into God's protective care and love.

3. Imagine going back in time to before you were born. Back to that time when you were developing in your mother's womb. What names for God come to mind from that period of your life? Speak those names aloud, if you are comfortable doing so.

4. Imagine the moment when you are born into this world and experiencing life as an infant. What names for God come to you from this period of your life?

5. Now you are in your early childhood. How do you experience God? What is the relationship like to you? What names do you give to God?

6. You are off to school and more grown now, approaching your teen years. How does God seem to encounter you now? What names would you give to God?

7. You have moved into your adolescent years. Who or what is God like for you at this time in your life? What names do you use?

8. As a young adult many new tasks and discoveries are occurring. Where is God for you now? What metaphors might describe your experience of God at this time in your life?

9. You now journey into your thirties and forties. Take a moment to be in touch with what names you use or want to use to express your relationship to God at this time in your life.

10. Now you are in your fifties and sixties, fully matured as an adult. What names come to mind pointing to your relationship with God at this age?

11. In your seventies and older. . . . What names do you give to God?

12. At the time of your death. . . . What names do you give to God?

13. On the other side of life. . . . What names do you imagine saying for God?[2]

4. Prayerfulness Exercise

1. Invite the group into a time of prayer, asking people to move into personal prayer.

2. Ask them to notice what happens for them as they pray.

3. After a time, ask those who are praying with their eyes closed to open them and continue in prayer—noticing the differences and similarities in their prayer while praying.

4. After a time, ask people to connect with a partner and talk to each other about what is happening to them in this situation—while continuing to maintain a sense of being in prayer during the sharing.

5. After a time, ask the group to discuss this experience with each other—while continuing to maintain a sense of being in prayer during the discussion.

6. Close the formal time of prayer, inviting a continuing sense of prayerfulness throughout the meeting.[3]

5. The Word of the Lord Came to Me: Guided Imagery Meditation

Now the word of the Lord came to me saying, "Before I formed you in the womb I knew you, and before you were born I consecrated you; I appointed you a prophet to the nations." Then I said, "Ah, Lord God! Truly I do not know how to speak, for I am only a boy."

*But the L*ORD *said to me, "Do not say, 'I am only a boy'; for you shall go to all to whom I send you, and you shall speak whatever I command you. Do not be afraid of them, for I am with you to deliver you, says the L*ORD*." Then the L*ORD *put out his hand and touched my mouth; and the L*ORD *said to me, "Now I have put my words in your mouth. See, today I appoint you over nations and over kingdoms, to pluck up and to pull down, to destroy and to overthrow, to build and to plant."*

—Jeremiah 1:4–10

1. Take a moment to invite God to be with you in this meditation, guiding you in this time of prayerful meditation, and opening you to a deeper relationship with the Holy One.

2. Imagine that you are in a special place where you feel most connected to God, to your deepest truest sense of yourself, and to the world around you. Perhaps it is a place you go to for rest and renewal . . . or worship . . . or vacation. Maybe it is a place that is known to you only in your imagination. Get as full a sense of being in that place as you are able, noticing what the place looks like and feeling yourself there. If there are other people there in that place, feel free to acknowledge them.

3. Now imagine that the Christ or the Spirit or the Holy Wisdom is also in that place. The Holy One might appear to you as someone you know, male or female, or as someone you imagine from art or some other source. The Holy One might take some other form than a human being . . . perhaps a special light, or sense of warmth, or an angelic form, or as a voice or music. Imagine that the Holy One wishes to come near you and seeks your consent to approach you. Do you give consent?

4. If you consent to the Holy One drawing close to you, notice how you feel as the Holy One approaches. . . . Listen as the Holy One tells you, "Before I formed you in the womb I knew you, and before you were born I consecrated you." Notice how you experience those words . . . what you feel and what thoughts arise in response to the Holy One telling you this.

5. Now the Holy One has something for you. It may be a word or phrase, or a symbol of some kind. It may be a sound or music or a gesture. . . . Receive whatever the Holy One has for you and feel free to ask questions and respond in any way you feel is appropriate or necessary.

6. The time has come to return to your normal consciousness...so say goodbye to the Holy One in whatever way seems fitting. Watch as the Holy One moves away from you, and the sense of the special place begins to fade. When you are ready, conclude this depth prayer by opening your eyes and joining us.

6. The Word That Speaks to Us Now

1. By memory, make a random listing of the words, phrases, and passages that have special meaning for you. If you cannot remember the exact words, use what you can remember. You will want to place on this list things that have sustained you in the past, or given you hope, or helped shape the direction of your religious journey. These can be favorite sayings, phrases or lines from hymns, liturgies, or Scripture, or quotations from others. Make the list as long as possible within the allotted time (perhaps 30 minutes).

2. Go back over your list now. Pick out the items that have special meaning to you at this moment. Which one speaks to the way you have been feeling most recently? (5 minutes)

3. Your top three choices may be an indication of where you are currently in your spiritual journey. Using this material, take time now to write a few lines describing your current journey. What makes these passages particularly significant to you now? How do they relate to the issues you are currently facing in your life? How do they relate to your past? Can you use the material to project into future dimensions of your pilgrimage? Give your interpretation of the meaning of your top three choices. (10 minutes)[4]

7. Jesus Blesses the Children

People were bringing little children to him in order that he might touch them. . . .
—Mark 10:13–16

Imagine that you are a little child again, wanting to go to Jesus. There is a crowd around him. Some in the crowd are children and some are adults. You see him pick up children and give them hugs and say prayers of blessing. The children are deeply cared for in his presence.

As you get closer to him, notice if you are coming to him by yourself or if there is someone, an adult or a child, who is with you. In your imagination you can bring in some caring friend or guide to be with you if you feel the need. Notice any thoughts and feelings you have. If you need to talk to a friend or guide, feel free to do so.

. . . and the disciples spoke sternly to them.

You are nearly with Jesus when some adult (or adults) tries to stop you. Who is creating a barrier or block between you and Jesus' blessing? What is that person or group of people saying and doing that is attempting to keep you from Jesus' (God's) love and blessing? Pay attention to how you feel and what you think about this. Again, if you need to talk to a caring friend or guide in your imagination, do so.

But when Jesus saw this, he was indignant and said to them, "Let the little children come to me; do not stop them; for it is to such as these that the kingdom of God belongs. Truly I tell you, whoever does not receive the kingdom of God as a little child will never enter it."

Jesus sees the activity that is holding you back from his grace and acts as a strong advocate for you. Nothing and no one can keep you from him. Listen to what he says to those who would try to keep you from him. See how they must open up for you the pathway to him. The kingdom of God belongs to you. It is yours as a good gift. Pay attention to your thoughts and feelings.

And he took them up in his arms,
laid his hands on them, and blessed them.

Take as much time as you need to receive God's love and blessing. God is infinitely patient, but deeply desires to give you an abundance of love and blessing when you are willing to receive it. If you need to test the relationship with Jesus, do so. You can have a friend or guide. You need only do what feels safe to you. You may talk to Jesus. If you wish, you may touch him, if that feels safe to you. Jesus will tenderly hold you with respectful care and loving regard if you want him to.

However you interact with him, Jesus has a gift for you. It might be a word or phrase that is life-empowering. It might be a song or music that carries special significance. It might be a picture or some other symbol of your meeting. Receive his gift and go with his blessing. Know that you can return to him whenever you desire or need to. For to you belongs the kingdom of God.

8. Meditation on the Body of Christ

St. Paul uses the metaphor of the human body several times in his letters to suggest that the quality of belonging among members of the Christian community is that of being parts of one whole body that is Christ.

We are going to explore that image of relationships in this community. But first, let's quiet ourselves and honor our own bodies.

1. Take a little time to pay attention to your body. . . . Your faithful body keeps you alive and aware and maturing. If it could speak to you, what might it tell you? Let's see.

2. Scan your body and notice the places of tension, and constriction. Imagine a sense of Christ's healing and warm light going to those places. With your inhalation, imagine the Spirit moving to those places to free them up and relax them. On your exhalation, imagine the Spirit collecting the tension and hurt and anxiety and carrying it out of your body to be used by God. If you wish to place your hand on a tense or hurting part of your body and imagine Jesus' healing touch, feel free to do so.

3. Now scan your body to notice those places of particular energy and power. Imagine the Spirit of Christ blessing and empowering them as gifts for you and for the world. With your breath, imagine the Spirit moving to those places in your body and exulting in their aliveness. If you wish, put your hand on that place on your body, imaging Jesus' empowering and liberating touch blessing you.

4. Listen now to what St. Paul wrote in the fourth chapter of his letter to the church in Ephesus:

> I therefore, the prisoner in the Lord, beg you to lead a life worthy of the calling to which you have been called, with all humility and gentleness, with patience, bearing with one another in love, making every effort to maintain the unity of the Spirit in the bond of peace. There is one body and one Spirit, just as you were called to the one hope of your calling, one Lord, one faith, one baptism, one God and Father of all, who is above all and through all and in all. But each of us was given grace according to the measure of Christ's gift....
>
> The gifts he gave were that some would be apostles, some prophets, some evangelists, some pastors and teachers, to equip the saints for the work of ministry, for building up the body of Christ, until all of us come to the unity of the faith and of the knowledge of the Son of God, to maturity, to the measure of the full stature of Christ. We must no longer be children, tossed to and fro and blown about by every wind of doctrine, by people's trickery, by their craftiness in deceitful scheming. But speaking the truth in love, we must grow up in every way into him who is the head, into Christ, from whom the whole body, joined and knit properly together by every ligament with which it is equipped, as each part is working properly, promotes the body's growth in building itself up in love. (Eph. 4:1-7, 11–16)

5. Now open your eyes for a moment and notice this gathering of Christ's community. Do not speak or move, simply notice us here— brought together in the wonderful mystery of Christ's calling. Then close your eyes again and bring the image of our community into your imagination, your inner world.

6. Imagine Christ's Spirit radiating within and around us all. Imagine that a divine energy made of God's breath and light and love permeates our group, bonding us together. Notice how you experience this, what feelings and thoughts come to your awareness. Being in this group does not diminish you. Rather, your life is enhanced. You do not diminish others in the group. Rather, you seek their fulfillment.

7. You have gifts that are brought out and received by the group with respect and joy. Become aware of those gifts that you have to share.... Others in the group also have gifts to share with you. Notice what those gifts are and perhaps who is giving the

gift.... Imagine a time of sharing gifts among the group. Notice your thoughts and feelings. And how you express them.

8. Become aware once more of your breathing. Your faithful body keeps you alive and aware and maturing. Listen now to the sound of the bell [or other signal], calling you gently to leave your inner world and join us as a member of this community, taking your part in the body of Christ.

9. Listening to Our Bodies as Messengers of God

Lord, you have searched me out and known me;
*   you know my sitting down and my rising up;*
*   you discern my thoughts from afar.*
You trace my journeys and my resting-places
*   and are acquainted with all my ways.*
Indeed, there is not a word on my lips,
*   but you, O Lord, know it all together.*
You press upon me behind and before
*   and lay your hand upon me.*
Such knowledge is too wonderful for me;
*   it is so high that I cannot attain to it....*
For you yourself created my inmost parts;
*   you knit me together in my mother's womb.*
I will thank you because I am marvelously made;
*   your works are wonderful, and I know it well.*
My body was not hidden from you,
*   while I was being made in secret*
*   and woven in the depths of the earth.*
Your eyes beheld my limbs, yet unfinished in the womb;
*   all of them were written in your book;*
they were fashioned day by day,
*   when as yet there were none of them.*
*   —Psalm 139:1–5, 12–15[5]*

1. With your feet firmly on the ground, or lying down comfortably, relax ever more deeply with each breath.... Think of your inhalation as God's breathing the Spirit into you. And your exhalation as offering yourself into God's care and love.... With

each breath in, imagine the light of the Spirit radiating energy and health to each part of your body. With each breath out, imagine the Spirit carrying out any stresses and toxins and concerns you have. Take a few minutes to relax into the intimate love and care of God's grace for you.

2. Now let your prayerful awareness scan your entire body. Do some places in your body feel constricted or tense or uncomfortable? Listen with love and compassion to those places of discomfort. Perhaps a thought or image comes to your mind about what that place of tension or hurt wants to tell you about itself and the cause of its discomfort. Listen to your body's wisdom about what might bring you new relief and healing.... Imagine the Spirit flooding that uncomfortable part of your body with healing light, or imagine Jesus placing a warm healing hand upon that place. If you are comfortable doing so, place your own hand prayerfully on that place of discomfort, adding your own consent to God's healing presence. Releasing the constriction or hurt...relaxing the tissue ...surrounding the cause of the discomfort with God's wise and protective care for you.... If there are other places of constriction or discomfort, go to those places in your prayerful awareness and again listen with compassion to what they might say to you; then invite the Spirit's healing light, or Jesus' and perhaps your own healing touch.

3. Now let your awareness again scan your body, resting on those places that feel particularly awakened and alive and gifted.... Listen to what those places in your body wish to tell you about your life.... Let the Spirit flood those places too with light—this time rejoicing at your empowerment—or imagine Jesus placing a hand of blessing; if you are comfortable doing so, put your own hand on those places and add your own consent to God's blessing.... Again, let your awareness go to any other place on your body that calls for attention...listen to its story and wisdom...and invite the Spirit's light or Jesus' blessing or healing hand, and add your own touch of consent to God's healing or blessing if you are comfortable doing so.

4. We have come to the end of our time in this depth prayer, this meditation. Remember what you have heard from the wisdom of your body. It is God's messenger to you. And now, take a few additional holy breaths, and slowly turn your attention to the outer world where we are present with you.[6]

10. Lending Your Eyes to Christ

Imagine that for the next few minutes you are lending your eyes to Christ. But this is not just an imaginative exercise; rather, practice this as a form of prayer, imagining that God sees the world through your eyes, looking where you look, seeing what you see. In your sharing the world that you see with God, notice any changes that you experience in your feelings and thoughts about what you see.

11. Meeting the Inner Wise One

Wisdom has built her house, she has hewn her seven pillars,
She has slaughtered her animals,
    she has mixed her wine, she has also set her table.
She has sent out her servant-girls,
    she calls from the highest places in the town,
    "You that are simple, turn in here!"
To those without sense she says, "Come, eat of my bread
    and drink of the wine I have mixed.
Lay aside immaturity, and live,
    and walk in the way of insight."
                  —Proverbs 9:1–6

1. Close your eyes, if you are comfortable doing so, and imagine you are in a green meadow.

2. Look around and notice what you see and feel. Notice how the ground feels below your feet.

3. Notice that there is a narrow dirt path that leads up a small hill. Walk on that path, up the hill, to the place where the Wise One stays.

4. When you reach the door to the house of the Wise One, knock at the door and enter when you are bidden to do so.

5. Look around the room and look at the Wise One. What do you see in the room? Who or what does the Wise One look like to you?

6. You may have a question for the Wise One or you might wish to tell the Wise One about something that you are now considering. Ask the Wise One's counsel on whatever you wish, and listen for his or

her reply. If you need further clarifications, feel free to engage in further conversation with the Wise One.

7. The Wise One says that she or he has something for you. It might be a special word or phrase for you to take with you, or an object, or a song or some other gift. Receive the gift the Wise One has for you, and feel free to ask about it if you need to know more. Respond to the Wise One's gift in whatever way you think is appropriate.

8. It is now time to say farewell to the Wise One. Do so, and then go to the door... walk down the hill on the path... and to the meadow, ... remembering your time with the Wise One and the gift you received, knowing also that you can visit your inner Wise One again. Whenever you are ready, open your eyes and bring your attention back to your outer world and this place.

12. Praying For and With a Guiding Symbol

1. Invite the group into a time of silent prayer (may or may not have background instrumental music) that is asking God for guiding symbols for the group (or for the larger community) for this time in its life. The symbols that emerge might include such things as: a passage or scene from Scripture; a word or phrase from some other wisdom source; a song; an image; or a wisdom person from the spiritual tradition. In the prayer time the pray-er may imaginatively engage the emerging symbol in any way that seems appropriate. If a symbol does not emerge for some members, ask them simply to stay with the quality of the emptiness.

2. Open and close the period of silent group contemplative prayer simply, perhaps using a bell, chant, or other audible signal.

3. Following the extended silence, invite the group members to share what emerged for them as guiding symbols or qualities of emptiness, and let the group reflect upon what was received from God to provide guidance to the community.

13. Those Who Have Been Christ for You

1. There may have been people in your life who have led you to a greater wholeness in your life. This is a time for you to take a moment to appreciate those people and give thanks for the way they touched your life. They have represented the way Christ would be to you—and in some ways they have been Christ's presence for you.

2. So open your heart and mind and let the memories and images of these people come to you from over your lifetime—from your childhood to the present day:

    The person who showed you unconditional love ...

    The person who was a healing presence for you in a time of deep hurting ...

    The person who showed you a more joyful way to live ...

    The person who forgave you ...

    The person who pointed the way for you when you did not know what to do or where to go.

3. Take a moment to savor their presence in your life and give thanks to God for giving them to you.

4. Are there ways that they have touched you that you can bring to someone else now? Are there ways you might represent Christ's presence and love to someone in your life? Who might that be? What might that person need from you? Are you willing to pray that God equips you to serve that person?

14. What Name Do You Give God?

Nikos Kazantzakis and Abbé Mugnier are companions walking on a road to Knossos, Crete. They stop for a rest at a monastery occupied by dervishes and engage one of them in conversation. The dervish says ...

"If a man cannot dance, he cannot pray. Angels have mouths but lack the power of speech. They speak to God by dancing."

"Father, what name do you give God?" asked the abbé.

"God does not have a name," the dervish replied. "He is too big to fit inside names. A name is a prison, God is free."

"But in case you should want to call Him," the abbé persisted, "when there is need, what name will you use?"

The dervish bowed his head and thought. Finally he parted his lips: "Ah!—that is what I shall call Him. Not Allah, but Ah!"

This troubled the abbé. "He's right," he murmured.[7]

Islamic prayer beads consist of thirty-three beads, and one devotional practice is to go around the circle of beads three times reciting the ninety-nine names for God. (It is reported that there actually are one hundred names for God, but only the camel knows the one hundredth and it isn't telling anyone.)

How many names do you have for God? What names have you heard others say that speak of the attributes of God?

[If you have some form of prayer beads, pass them from person to person, asking that when they receive the beads they say a name or attribute for God. Continue this around the group for a while. If you do not have prayer beads, you can ask people randomly to give names they have heard for God. Sometimes I write the names that are said on a marker board for all to see.]

What is the name you use now, or would like to use, at this time in your life, that expresses your relationship with God? Is this name for the Divine consistent with your desired relationship with God?

15. Discovering the Community's Treasure

The kingdom of heaven is like treasure hidden in a field, which someone found and hid; then in his joy he goes and sells all that he has and buys that field.

—Matthew 13:44

Ask people to move into a prayerful and quiet state.

1. Invite the group to imagine that they are at a warm beach together. Notice the place . . . it may be a special place that you visit, or it might be a new location. . . . Feel the sand on your feet. Notice the color of the water and size of the waves. What does the sky look

like? Cloudy? Clear? Take in the scene with as much detail as you are able and put yourself there physically as much as you can. Notice everyone else who is with you, too. You might invite the Christ to come and join you, also. If so, notice how the Christ appears to you, and as a group extend a greeting. . . .

2. You have the chance to go together on a treasure hunt, looking for a box or chest of treasure that is somewhere on the beach. Look around for the treasure until someone finds the box or chest. . . . Then everyone goes to the treasure. . . . If it is partially buried, dig it out of the sand. . . . Notice the details of the box or chest. . . . Then do whatever is necessary to open the container. . . .

3. When the container is opened, you and the group are free to take the treasure out and look it over. . . . What is the treasure of this group? What are the symbols that represent the treasure of this community? Freely interact in discussion about the treasure with members of your group—and with the Christ, if the Christ is present. . . .

4. Now it is time to begin your journey back. As a group, you are free to bring the treasure with you. If the Christ is with you, thank the Christ for being present. Again feel the sand beneath your feet. . . . Then slowly come out of your inner meditation and join us in this place.[8]

16. Praying with an Icon or Other Subject of Art or Nature

1. Take time to quiet down and be open to the possibility of the sacred dimension of life being known in a new way through this subject.

2. Gaze at the subject as if it were a window into sacred reality.

3. Notice what holds your attention after you have scanned everything. Where does it carry your thoughts and/or feelings? Are memories or situations evoked? Is this an invitation to a particular prayer focus?

4. If the subject could speak to you, what might he/she/it have to say to you about what is occurring in your life? What might you ask and dialogue about?

5. Are there characteristics of the subject that you might be invited to receive as a gift from God?

6. What do you need to do or be right now to be a friend of this "friend of God"? Do it.

7. How might this friend of God (behind the representation) pray for you? Can you ask your friend to pray for you? Can you pray for this friend?

17. Spirit's Presence, Christ's Mind (Group)

Now we have received not the spirit of the world, but the Spirit that is from God, so that we may understand the gifts bestowed on us by God. And we speak of these things in words not taught by human wisdom but taught by the Spirit. . . . "For who has known the mind of the Lord so as to instruct him?" But we have the mind of Christ.
—1 Corinthians 2:12–13a, 16

Offer some preliminary comments about visualizing the Spirit of Christ.

1. In your imagination, try to visualize this gathering. Try to re-create the outward reality of this group and this place in your inner world in as much detail as possible, including the sounds you are now hearing, the people, the room. . . .

2. Imagine that the Spirit of Christ wants to be with us and now enters your vision. Notice how you feel about the Spirit of Christ wanting to be with you and this group. Notice in what form the Spirit of Christ appears to you.

3. Greet the Spirit of Christ in whatever way seems appropriate to you.

4. You have the chance to bring to Christ whatever question or concern or need for guidance about the group's deliberations and your feelings about it that you wish, and to seek Christ's response. Listen and watch for Christ's guidance. It may come to you as a word or phrase, a song, or a symbol. Feel free to discuss the meaning of this with Christ or invite others in the group to help you understand Christ's guidance.

5. The time has come for this meditation to end. How do you want to end this time with the Spirit of Christ's visit? Let the group express their thanks for the Spirit's willingness to be present in this depth prayer.

6. Begin to become increasingly aware of your outer world and gently shift your attention from the inner to our external gathering.

18. The Face of Christ

There is a Russian Orthodox liturgical greeting rather like the exchange of the peace in Western worship. The greeting is, "In your eyes I see the face of Christ."

Using this greeting silently and repetitively as a meditation focus, go into a setting where you will have contact with people. In your encounters with each person, notice how the silently repeated greeting of "In your eyes I see the face of Christ" affects your relationship with them.

19. Resurrection Appearance to the Disciples

Patterned on John 20:19–22 or Luke 24:36b–40, 44–49

The meditation should allow frequent pauses for people to visualize or think through different scenes. This meditation is designed for the group to focus particularly on how Christ might engage us as a Christian community rather than as individuals. It could be modified to focus attention on the individual perspective.

1. Imagine your congregation [or church leaders] is gathered together in a particular place [for a meeting to try to answer an important question].

2. Imagine the resurrected Christ appearing in the midst of the gathering. What does the Christ look like? How do you feel about Christ's presence? What about others in your church? Is anyone saying anything or doing anything in response to Christ's appearing?

3. Are there things that your church community is afraid of or concerned about or seeks direction about that needs to be brought

to Christ? What does Christ say or do about your fears or concerns or request for direction?

4. Christ offers you peace. What is that like for you and the rest of the community?

5. Christ empowers your community to a mission beyond yourselves. What might that be? What does it feel like to receive the power of the Spirit? What gifts or abilities seem to emerge for your community's empowerment? Are you aware of resistance or confusion or other barriers to receiving this empowerment? If so, you can ask Christ for guidance.

6. You might ask the Christ for a word or phrase or gift that speaks to the nature of your community at this time. Receive whatever Christ has to give you on behalf of your community. Ask whatever questions you need to for understanding this word, phrase, or gift.

7. The time has come for you to say goodbye and return from the meditation with your memories of this encounter. Say your farewell in any way that feels appropriate.

[Provide an opportunity for the group to debrief.]

20. Questions for a Church

Based on Matthew 22:2–14, the Parable of the King's Marriage Feast for his Son

Invite the group into a contemplative silence in preparation for reading the parable. Then read the parable slowly and clearly. Ask people to consider the following questions quietly. Either read them slowly to the group, giving time for people to notice what comes to mind, or hand out the questions to them and ask them to take notes on what emerges for them.

After going through the questions, ask for people's responses and allow time for the members of the group to reflect together.

1 Is there some authority equivalent to the king in this church?

2. Who operates as the servants to the king here?

3. What goes on here that is worthy of sending out an invitation to others? Is there some equivalent of a royal wedding banquet or a

feast or something else that is celebrated? What is this church's particular Good News?

4. How have invitations been sent out in the past, and how are they being sent out now?

5. Who is designated to send out invitations? Are they equipped and authorized to send out invitations?

6. To whom have the invitations been addressed? In other words, who is selected to receive an invitation? Who decides who gets selected? What are their replies?

7. Who is *not* invited? Why are they not invited? Is there a need or concern that the church has that discourages membership of particular groups of people?

8. What do the invitations say about this particular church and its Good News? Do the invitations accurately represent the church?

9. What is the mood or atmosphere of this church in its worship, preaching, teaching, and ministries?

10. Does the behavior seem consistent with its understanding of its purpose for being here?

11. Are its people challenged to grow into deeper Christian maturity and joy? Are there adequate supports for them to continue to grow?

21. Draw Your Mandala

Bring a picture of a mandala to show the group. You will need to have drawing materials on hand for this exercise.

People of many cultures create mandalas as symbols of wholeness. Usually a mandala includes a large circle, and often it presents some display of four directions or quadrants. This exercise is an opportunity for you to create your own mandala—some symbolic representation of what wholeness is like for you. It may or may not include a circle or four directions/quadrants. Create it in any way you feel best represents your own sense of wholeness and what is included in bringing that about.[9]

22. Take a Contemplative Walk

For this group exercise form, invite everyone to take a walk together quietly, especially if you are in an urban area. Ask that people not talk to each other, but gently and slowly walk over a particular route that you set for them (perhaps around a city block, or to a park and back). Ask that they stay prayerfully open and accepting of whatever sights and sounds come their way, noticing what they evoke within them. This can be an opportunity to encounter God in the concreteness of an outdoor situation. An alternative if people are in a retreat setting is to allow them a particular time to wander as they will on the retreat grounds and then return to the group at the appointed time. In either situation, invite sharing in the group following the walk.

23. *Darshan*: The Holy Gaze

The holy gaze is a practice in Hindu meditation between the student and the guru. However, we can adapt it to other spiritual perspectives as well. For instance, in the Episcopal Church's renewal of baptismal vows we ask people if they promise to seek and serve Christ in each other, loving their neighbors as themselves.

In this exercise members of the group divide into pairs and sit wordlessly gazing into each other's faces for an extended period of time. They are asked to notice feelings that come and go. Do they get a glimpse of the Holy One in the face of the other person? If so, what is that like? After a period of gazing, provide the pairs a chance to share with each other and then provide a chance for group reflection on the experience.

24. Life Symbol Meditation

For this individual meditation you may go outside and explore the world of creation or go to a quiet place inside the building and journey within. Be open to receiving something that is symbolic of where you are in your life right now.

Let the symbol or image or natural object choose you, emerge from a deep place within you, speak to you. Bring the symbol back with you from outdoors, or draw it using art supplies, or write a haiku or other short poem about it. At the designated time bring the emergent symbol with you to your group.

25. Scripture Role Play

1. Introduce the Scripture passage, providing a basic context.

2. Have someone read the passage aloud.

3. Ask the group to identify the characters, buildings, and objects in the biblical scene.

4. Invite group members to associate themselves with a particular character or object in the scene and have one person become the reader/narrator (if called for in the passage).

5. Ask the group members to re-create the passage with everyone speaking or acting in their role (including inanimate objects like a street, tree, mountain, and so on), led by the narrator.

6. Debrief the experience, with each person sharing from his or her unique perspective. (What was it like for you to be ... ?)

7. Discuss any questions and insights that may arise related to the group as a whole and/or a member's particular situation.[10]

26. A Spiritual Timeline

Invite participants to draw a line on paper and divide the line into decades in their lives. Along that timeline they will place a mark and make a note to describe the time when a significant situation occurred that affected or shaped their spiritual life. The situation could be perceived as positive or negative. After they have placed marks and made their notes, invite them to re-gather and share stories of one or two of those significant events and how those events have helped shape their spiritual lives.

27. Four Elements Meditation

1. Begin with a chant such as *O Great Spirit* or *Gather Us, O God.*

2. Have placed in the center a lit candle, a feather, a rock, and a container of water, equally spaced.

3. Describe our selves as a complex unity of being: body, spirit, soul, and mind.

4. Give an invitation to honor the various dimensions of our lives, and listen for needs and movements toward greater wholeness.

5. Introduce each element, one at a time, and name some possible meanings of each symbol, inviting participants to consider that other meanings might emerge for them as the element is passed to each participant.

6. Some possible meanings:
   Candlelight/fire: illumination, mind, clarity, study, purification by fire, burning, passionate aspiration, knowledge, guidance
   Feather: Spirit, freedom, high vision, lightness, soaring, cannot be contained, wild
   Rock: body, material, down-to-earth, earthiness, stability, hardness, strength, structure
   Container of water: baptism, need for purification, mystery, depths, well, soul-dimension, descent, loss, grieving

7. Allow quiet reflection time (soft music in background), letting the participants reflect on what is evoked for them about their life situation. They may hold any of the elements as they meditate upon them.

8. Participants may consider how the symbol has meaning for them in their life right now. Does it evoke a situation of grace or of need? A situation where there is positive or negative energy?

9. After the period of quiet meditation is over, ask participants to return to the circle to reflect together. Invite them, if they wish, to take an element to talk about. Does one element/dimension speak particularly strongly to them about a need or thanksgiving that they wish to mention and/or take to prayer? Is there some need for balance? Some movement to greater wholeness called forth?[11]

28. Lamb and Lion Within

Note the peaceful kingdom of Isaiah 11, and that Jesus referred to both a lion and a lamb in Revelation 5.

Various wisdom traditions speak of powerful inner energies that are polarities but can be integrated and lead to greater wholeness. One of the energies might be thought of as a lamb. It is soft and gentle; it is an energy of desire and attraction. It wishes to merge or be at one with others or other things. The other energy might be thought of as a lion. It is fierce and powerful. It is an energy of strength and anger, a warrior. It acts against that which does not feel right; or is unjust, or threatens well-being.

1. What do you associate in your life situation or experience with the lamb?

2. What do you associate in your life situation or experience with the lion?

3. Do you need more of one or the other energy in your life right now? Do they feel like they serve you and God and your community well at this time, or are adjustments needed?

Bibliography

Anonymous. *The Cloud of Unknowing and The Book of Privy Counseling.* Edited and Introduction by William Johnston. Garden City, N.Y.: Image Books, 1973.

Arnold, Jeffrey. *Small Group Outreach: Turning Groups Inside Out.* Downers Grove: InterVarsity Press, 1998.

Benner, David G. *Sacred Companions: The Gift of Spiritual Friendship and Direction.* Downers Grove: InterVarsity Press, 2002.

Bion, W. R. *Experiences in Groups: And Other Papers.* New York: Ballantine Books, 1974.

Bloom, Anthony. *Beginning to Pray.* Mahwah, N.J.: Paulist Press, 1970.

Bohler, Carolyn Stahl. *Opening to God: Guided Imagery Meditation on Scripture.* Revised edition. Nashville: The Upper Room, 1996.

Bourgeault, Cynthia. *Centering Prayer and Inner Awakening.* Cambridge, Mass.: Cowley Publications, 2004.

Brockman, Pat. C., O.S.U., Ph.D. *The Community Dream: Awakening the Christian Tribal Consciousness.* Boulder: WovenWord Press, 2000.

Brooke, Avery. *Healing in the Landscape of Prayer.* Cambridge, Mass.: Cowley Publications, 1996.

————. *Learning and Teaching Christian Meditation*. Revised edition. Cambridge, Mass.: Cowley Publications, 1990.

Brother Lawrence of the Resurrection. *The Practice of the Presence of God*. Translated by Ronald Attwater. Introduction by Dorothy Day. Springfield, Ill.: Templegate, 1974.

Brown, Robert McAfee. *Spirituality and Liberation: Overcoming the Great Fallacy*. Louisville: Westminster Press, 1988.

Broz, Mary Ruth, R.S.M., and Barbara Flynn. *Midwives of an Unnamed Future: Spirituality for Women in Times of Unprecedented Change*. Chicago: ACTA Publications, 2006.

Bulkeley, Kelly. *Transforming Dreams: Learning Spiritual Lessons from the Dreams You Never Forget*. New York: John Wiley & Sons, 2000.

————. *The Wilderness of Dreams: Exploring the Religious Meanings of Dreams in Modern Western Culture*. Albany: State University of New York Press, 1994.

Canham, Elizabeth J. *Heart Whispers: Benedictine Wisdom for Today*. Nashville: The Upper Room, 1999.

Chittister, Joan D., O.S.B. *The Rule of Benedict: Insights for the Ages*. New York: Crossroads, 1997.

————. *Wisdom Distilled from the Daily*. San Francisco: HarperCollins, 1991.

Cloud, Henry, and John Townsend. *Making Small Groups Work: What Every Small Group Leader Needs to Know*. Grand Rapids: Zondervan, 2003.

Coughlin, Patricia, O.S.B. "Dreamsharing and Communal Conversion." D.Min. thesis, Christian Theological Seminary, Chicago, Illinois. June 2002.

De Mello, Anthony. *Sadhana, A Way to God: Christian Exercises in Eastern Form*. Garden City, N.Y.: Image Books, 1984.

De Waal, Esther. *A Life-Giving Way: A Commentary on the Rule of St. Benedict*. Collegeville: The Liturgical Press, 1995.

————. *Seeking God: The Way of St. Benedict*. Collegeville: The Liturgical Press, 2001.

————. *To Pause at the Threshold: Reflections on Living on the Border*. Harrisburg: Morehouse Publishing, 2001.

DeYoung, Curtiss Paul. *Living Faith: How Faith Inspires Social Justice.* Minneapolis: Fortress Press, 2007.

Donahue, Bill. *Leading Life-Changing Small Groups.* Revised edition. Grand Rapids: Zondervan, 2002.

Donahue, Bill, and Russ G. Robinson. *Building a Church of Small Groups: A Place Where Nobody Stands Alone.* Grand Rapids: Zondervan, 2001.

Dougherty, Rose Mary, S.S.N.D. *Group Spiritual Direction: Community for Discernment.* Mahwah, N.J.: Paulist Press, 1995.

Dougherty, Rose Mary, S.S.N.D., ed., with Monica Maxon and Lynne Smith. *The Lived Experience of Group Spiritual Direction.* Mahwah, N.J.: Paulist Press, 2003.

Dyckman, Katherine Marie, S.N.J.M., and L. Patrick Carroll, S.J. *Inviting the Mystic, Supporting the Prophet: An Introduction to Spiritual Direction.* Mahwah, N.J.: Paulist Press, 1981.

Edwards, Tilden. *Living in the Presence: Spiritual Exercises to Open Our Lives to the Awareness of God.* New York: HarperCollins, 1995.

Farnham, Suzanne G., Joseph P. Gill, R. Taylor McLean, and Susan M. Ward. *Listening Hearts: Discerning Call in Community.* Revised edition. Harrisburg: Morehouse Publishing, 1991.

Farnham, Suzanne G., Stephanie A. Hull, and R. Taylor McLean. *Grounded in God: Listening Hearts Discernment for Group Deliberations.* Revised edition. Harrisburg: Morehouse Publishing, 1999.

Friedman, Edwin H. *Generation to Generation: Family Process in Church and Synagogue.* New York: The Guilford Press, 1985.

Fryling, Alice. *Seeking God Together: An Introduction to Group Spiritual Direction.* Downers Grove: InterVarsity Press, 2009.

Garfield, Patricia. *Creative Dreaming: Plan and Control Your Dreams to Develop Creativity, Overcome Fears, Solve Problems, and Create a Better Self.* New York: Fireside Book, 1974, 1995.

Green, Thomas H., S.J. *When the Well Runs Dry: Prayer Beyond the Beginnings.* Notre Dame: Ave Maria Press, 1982.

Grenz, Linda L., ed. *In Dialogue with Scripture: An Episcopal Guide to Studying the Bible.* Fourth edition. New York: Episcopal Church Center, 1998.

Halpin, Marlene. *Imagine That! Using Phantasy in Spiritual Direction.* Dubuque: William C. Brown Co., 1982.

Judy, Dwight H. *Christian Meditation and Inner Healing.* Akron, Ohio: Order of Saint Luke Publications, 2000.

Jung, Carl G. *Memories, Dreams, Reflections.* New York: Vintage Books, 1965.

Kardong, Terrence G. *Benedict's Rule: A Translation and Commentary.* Collegeville: The Liturgical Press, 1996.

Keating, Thomas. *Intimacy with God: An Introduction to Centering Prayer.* New York: Crossroad, 1996.

———. *Open Mind, Open Heart: The Contemplative Dimension of the Gospel.* New York: Continuum, 1996.

Kelsey, Morton T. *Healing and Christianity: A Classic Study.* Third edition. Minneapolis: Augsburg Press, 1995.

———. *God, Dreams, and Revelation: A Christian Interpretation of Dreams.* Revised and expanded edition. Minneapolis: Augsburg Press, 1991.

———. *The Other Side of Silence: Meditation for the Twenty-First Century.* Revised edition. Mahwah, N.J.: Paulist Press, 1997.

Kirkpatrick, Thomas G. *Small Groups in the Church: A Handbook for Creating Community.* Herndon, Va.: The Alban Institute, 2000.

Ladinsky, Daniel, trans. *The Gift: Poems by Hafiz, the Great Sufi Master.* New York: Penguin Compass, 1999.

Law, Eric H. F. *The Wolf Shall Dwell with the Lamb: A Spirituality for Leadership in a Multicultural Community.* St. Louis: Chalice Press, 1993.

Lawrence, W. Gordon. *Introduction to Social Dreaming: Transforming Thinking.* New York: Karnac, 2005.

Lawrence, W. Gordon, ed. *Experiences in Social Dreaming.* New York: Karnac, 2003.

———. *Social Dreaming @ Work.* New York: Karnac, 1998.

Lionberger, John. *Renewal in the Wilderness: A Spiritual Guide to Connecting with God in the Natural World.* Woodstock, Vt.: Skylight Paths, 2007.

Mabry, John R. *Faith Styles: Ways People Believe.* Harrisburg: Morehouse Publishing, 2006.

———. *Noticing the Divine: An Introduction to Interfaith Spiritual Guidance.* Harrisburg: Morehouse Publishing, 2006.

Main, John. *The Way of Unknowing: Expanding Spiritual Horizons Through Meditation.* Eugene, Ore.: Wipf & Stock Publishers, 2004.

May, Gerald G., M.D. *Pilgrimage Home: The Conduct of Contemplative Practice in Groups.* Mahwah, N.J.: Paulist Press, 1979.

———. *Will and Spirit: A Contemplative Psychology.* New York: Harper & Row, 1982.

McBride, Neal F. *How to Lead Small Groups.* Colorado Springs: Navpress, 1990.

McKay, Bobbie, and Lewis A. Musil. *Healing the Spirit: Stories of Transformation.* Allen, Tex.: Thomas More Association, 2000.

Mulholland, M. Robert, Jr. *Invitation to a Journey: A Road Map for Spiritual Formation.* Downers Grove: InterVarsity Press, 1993.

———. *Shaped by the Word: The Power of Scripture in Spiritual Formation.* Nashville: The Upper Room, 1985.

Palmer, Parker J. *A Hidden Wholeness: The Journey Toward an Undivided Life.* San Francisco: Jossey-Bass, 2004.

———. *Let Your Life Speak: Listening for the Voice of Vocation.* San Francisco: Jossey-Bass, 2000.

Peck, M. Scott, M.D. *The Different Drum: Community Making and Peace.* New York: Touchstone, 1988, 1998.

Pennington, M. Basil, O.C.S.O. *Centered Living: The Way of Centering Prayer.* New York: Image, 1988.

———. *Centering Prayer: Renewing an Ancient Christian Prayer Form.* New York: Doubleday, 1980.

Perry, Michael, ed. *Deliverance: Psychic Disturbances and Occult Involvement.* Second edition. London: SPCK, 1996.

Prechtel, Daniel. "A Christian Reawakening to the Dream." *Dream Network Journal* 19, no. 3 (Fall 2000): 22–24.

———. "To Have the Mind of Christ: Symbol Guidance and the Development of Communal Spiritual Discernment Processes for Parish Life, Mission, and Ministry." D.Min. thesis, Seabury-Western Theological Seminary, Evanston, Illinois, May 2002.

Rakoczy, Susan, I.H.M. *Great Mystics and Social Justice: Walking on the Two Feet of Love*. Mahwah, N.J.: Paulist Press, 2006.

Rohr, Richard. *Everything Belongs: The Gift of Contemplative Prayer*. New York: Crossroad, 1999.

Sanford, Agnes. *The Healing Light*. Plainfield, N.J.: Logos International, 1976.

Sanford, John A. *Dreams: God's Forgotten Language*. New York: Crossroad, 1982.

———. *The Kingdom Within: The Inner Meaning of Jesus' Sayings*. Revised edition. New York: HarperCollins, 1987.

Smith, Martin L. *The Word Is Very Near You: A Guide to Praying with Scripture*. Cambridge, Mass.: Cowley Publications, 1989.

Stewart, Columba, O.S.B. *Prayer and Community: The Benedictine Tradition*. Traditions of Christian Spirituality Series. Maryknoll, N.Y.: Orbis Books, 1998.

Taylor, Brian C. *Spirituality for Everyday Living: An Adaptation of the Rule of St. Benedict*. Collegeville: The Liturgical Press, 1989.

Taylor, Jeremy. *Where People Fly and Water Runs Uphill: Using Dreams to Tap the Wisdom of the Unconscious*. New York: Time Warner, 1992.

Tomaine, Jane. *St. Benedict's Toolbox: The Nuts and Bolts of Everyday Benedictine Living*. Harrisburg: Morehouse Publishing, 2005.

Vennard, Jane E. *Be Still: Designing and Leading Contemplative Retreats*. Herndon, Va.: The Alban Institute, 2000.

Vest, Norvene. *Preferring Christ: A Devotional Commentary on the Rule of St. Benedict*. Harrisburg: Morehouse Publishing, 2004.

Ward, Benedicta, S.L.G., trans. *The Sayings of the Desert Fathers: The Alphabetical Collection*. Kalamazoo: Cistercian Publications, 1975.

Ware, Corinne. *Discover Your Spiritual Type: A Guide to Individual and Congregational Growth*. Herndon, Va.: The Alban Institute, 1995.

Wink, Walter. *The Powers That Be: Theology for a New Millennium.* New York: Augsburg Fortress, 1998.

————. *Transforming Bible Study.* Nashville: Abingdon Press, 1988.

Wolfteich, Claire E. *Lord, Have Mercy: Praying for Justice with Conviction and Humility.* The Practices of Faith Series. San Francisco: Jossey-Bass, 2006.

Wuellner, Flora Slosson. *Prayer, Stress, and Our Inner Wounds.* Nashville: The Upper Room, 1985.

Wuthnow, Robert, ed. *"I Come Away Stronger": How Small Groups Are Shaping American Religion.* Grand Rapids: Eerdmans, 1994.

Endnotes

Introduction

1. In later reflection I realized that my parents had been sustained in their former church through their own rich experience of a small group in that church.

2. The Academy for Spiritual Formation is an ecumenical two-year certificate program of study operated through The Upper Room. More information can be found on the Academy's website at http://upperroom.org/academy/.

3. More information about Lamb & Lion Spiritual Guidance Ministries can be found on the website at http://www.llministries.com.

Chapter 1
The Power of Small Groups
for Spiritual Companionship

1. Robert Wuthnow, ed., *"I Come Away Stronger": How Small Groups Are Shaping American Religion* (Grand Rapids: Eerdmans, 1994), Appendix: Small Groups—A National Profile.

2. Wuthnow, *"I Come Away Stronger,"* 373.

3. Wuthnow, *"I Come Away Stronger,"* 374.

4. *The Spiritual Health of the Episcopal Church,* conducted by the Gallup Organization, Inc. for the Episcopal Church Center (New York: Episcopal Parish Services, 1990).

5. *The Spiritual Health of the Episcopal Church,* 17–18.

6. See, for example, Diana Butler Bass, *The Practicing Congregation: Imagining a New Old Church* (Herndon, Va.: Alban Publishing, 2004).

7. Kennon L. Callahan, *Twelve Keys to an Effective Church: Strategic Planning for Mission* (San Francisco: Jossey-Bass Publishers, 1983, 1997).

8. Bill Donahue, *Leading Life-Changing Small Groups*, revised edition (Grand Rapids: Zondervan, 2002), 28.

9. *The Sayings of the Desert Fathers: The Alphabetical Collection*, trans. Benedicta Ward, S.L.G. (Kalamazoo: Cistercian Publications, 1975), 139.

10. Ward, *Sayings of the Desert Fathers*, 154.

11. Ward, *Sayings of the Desert Fathers*, 103.

12. Ward, *Sayings of the Desert Fathers*, 230-231.

13. From Kenneth Leech, *Soul Friend: An Invitation to Spiritual Direction* (San Francisco: HarperSanFrancisco, 1992), 50.

14. See Diarmuid O'Laoghaire, S.J., "Soul-Friendship," in *Traditions of Spiritual Guidance*, ed. Lavinia Byrne (Collegeville: Liturgical Press, 1990), 36–38.

15. Leech, *Soul Friend*, 50.

16. Anonymous, *The Way of a Pilgrim and The Pilgrim Continues His Way*, trans. R. M. French (New York: HarperCollins, 1965), 10–11.

17. *The Book of Common Prayer* (1662), The Order for the Administration of the Lord's Supper, or Holy Communion. Bracketed portion is my addition.

18. For a much more thorough treatment of the Anglican tradition of spiritual direction I would suggest *Anglican Spiritual Direction* by Peter Ball (Cambridge, Mass.: Cowley Publications, 1998).

19. Douglas V. Steere, *Gleanings: A Random Harvest* (Nashville: The Upper Room, 1986), 83.

20. More information about Spiritual Directors International can be found on the website at http://sdiworld.org.

21. *The Book of Common Prayer* (New York: Church Hymnal, 1979), 305.

22. This sense of sacred Presence in the other person may have a loose parallel with the Hindi greeting or salutation *Namaste,* which can be interpreted as, "The God/Goddess/Spirit within me recognizes and honors the God/Goddess/Spirit within you." See http://healing.about.com/od/n/g/g_namaste.htm.

23. See the entry "Panentheism" in the *New World Encyclopedia* at http://www.newworldencyclopedia.org/entry/Panentheism, which summarizes two meanings of panentheism. One meaning is closer to pantheism, and the other maintains an ontological difference between God and the created order. The latter meaning is that to which I subscribe.

24. Quoted in Joan Chittister, O.S.B., *The Rule of Benedict: Insights for the Ages,* chap. 53 (New York: Crossroads, 1997), 140.

25. My statement given to students as program director of the Group Spiritual Companionship training program for the opening day, August 19, 2008.

26. Bernard of Clairvaux, Sermon 18 in *On the Song of Songs I*, vol. 1, in *The Works of Bernard of Clairvaux*, trans. Kilian Walsh (Kalamazoo: Cistercian Publications, 1971), 134, 136.

27. Corinne Ware, *Discover Your Spiritual Type: A Guide to Individual and Congregational Growth* (Bethesda, Md.: The Alban Institute, 1995).

28. Ware acknowledges building upon the late Urban T. Holmes's *A History of Christian Spirituality* in her work. Before Holmes, Martin Thornton encouraged spiritual directors to pay attention to the spiritual *attraits* that make up the personality and apophatic or kataphatic orientation of the directee. Rachel Hosmer also used Holmes's typology and added suggestions on how each of the spiritual paths might engage in social actions of compassion and justice. All of these people also suggest a synthetic, integrative path of *via media* (middle way) which draws dynamically upon the other paths. The chart included here is reprinted from *Discover Your Spiritual Type: A Guide to Individual and Congregational Growth* by Corinne Ware, with permission from the Alban Institute. Copyright © 1995 by The Alban Institute, Inc. Herndon, Virginia. All rights reserved.

29. Tilden Edwards, *Spiritual Friend: Reclaiming the Gift of Spiritual Direction* (Mahwah, N.J.: Paulist Press, 1980), 112–116.

30. John R. Mabry, *Faith Styles: Ways People Believe* (Harrisburg: Morehouse Publishing, 2006). Mabry uses the term "Jack Believers," from those who are called "Jack Mormons," because they believe in that faith but are unable to live within it. They are condemned by their faith as "backsliders" or "apostates." If the styles were six points around a circle it could be described as: Ethical Humanists–Jack Believers–Traditional Believers–Liberal Believers– Spiritual Eclectics–Religious Agnostics.

31. Kent Groff, "Using Howard Gardner's 'Multiple Intelligences' in Spiritual Direction," *Presence: The Journal of Spiritual Directors International* 4, no. 2 (May 1998): 17–24.

32. James W. Fowler, *Stages of Faith: The Psychology of Human Development and the Quest for Meaning* (San Francisco: Harper & Row, 1981). Robert Kegan, *The Evolving Self: Problem and Process in Human Development* (Cambridge, Mass.: Harvard University Press, 1982). From a spiritual direction perspective, I particularly recommend Elizabeth Liebert, S.N.J.M., *Changing Life Patterns: Adult Development in Spiritual Direction* (Mahwah, N.J.: Paulist Press, 1992).

33. See Morton Kelsey's *The Other Side of Silence: Meditation for the Twenty-First Century*, revised edition (Mahwah, N.J.: Paulist Press, 1997) and *God, Dreams, and Revelation: A Christian Interpretation of Dreams* (Minneapolis: Augsburg Fortress, 1991) for his most developed graphs and discussions of these interior realms.

34. Katherine Marie Dyckman, S.N.J.M., and L. Patrick Carroll, S.J., *Inviting the Mystic, Supporting the Prophet: An Introduction to Spiritual Direction* (Mahwah, N.J.: Paulist Press, 1981), 28-29.

Chapter 2:
Essentials of Spiritual
Companionship Groups

1. The word *contemplative* has many meanings. I particularly like the definition Tilden Edwards offers of "attention to our direct, loving, receptive, trusting presence for God. This attention includes the desire to be present through and beyond images, thoughts, and feelings." Tilden Edwards, *Living in the Presence: Spiritual Exercises to Open Our Lives to the Awareness of God* (New York: HarperCollins, 1994), 2.

Chapter 3:
Groups for Sharing
Spiritual Practices and Exercises

1. Mulholland introduced this in a presentation I attended through The Upper Room's Academy for Spiritual Formation #5 in May 1989. He subsequently developed the idea in a book, *Invitation to a Journey: A Road Map for Spiritual Formation* (Downers Grove: InterVarsity Press, 1993).

2. Adapted from "An Oral Tradition Method," *In Dialogue with Scripture,* ed. Linda L. Grenz, fourth edition (New York: Episcopal Church Center, 1998), 92–93.

3. From a Contemplative Outreach, Ltd. brochure that is downloadable at http://www.contemplativeoutreach.org/sites/default/files/documents/method cp2008.pdf.

4. John Main, *The Way of Unknowing: Expanding Spiritual Horizons Through Meditation* (Eugene, Ore.: Wipf & Stock Publishers, 1990), ix.

5. Edwards, *Living in the Presence,* 2.

Chapter 4:
Groups for Cultivating
Inner Awareness and Discernment

1. Interview conducted at Seabury-Western Theological Seminary in November 1998 for research about dreams and discernment. He is now a bishop in Sudan.

2. Thomas R. Kelly, *A Testament of Devotion* (New York: Harper & Row, 1941), 1.

3. Danny E. Morris and Charles M. Olsen, *Discerning God's Will Together: A Spiritual Practice for the Church* (Nashville: The Upper Room, 1997), 33.

4. Morris and Olsen, *Discerning God's Will Together,* 33.

5. Morris and Olsen, *Discerning God's Will Together,* 34–35.

6. See Rose Mary Dougherty, S.S.N.D., *Group Spiritual Direction: Community for Discernment* (Mahwah, N.J.: Paulist Press, 1995), 49–55, 98–100 for a full description of the process.

7. I am grateful for Suzanne Farnham's encouragement to a group of us in a diocesan Listening Hearts training week to let a question or an image "ripen" until it is mature and fully formed and timely. It took us out of an interior space of anxiety about getting our questions out before the thought was lost or the stream of exploration had moved away from our concern, and took us to a closer attentiveness to the Spirit at work, leading us in our companionship with the presenter.

8. From *The Psalter,* translated by the International Commission on English in the Liturgy (Chicago: Liturgy Training Publications, 1995).

9. Although I am using the word "level" for the following possible dimensions of meaning, I am not intending to imply a hierarchical or developmental structure.

10. Kelly Bulkeley, *The Wilderness of Dreams: Exploring the Religious Meaning of Dreams in Modern Western Culture* (Albany: State University of New York Press, 1994), 184.

11. Bulkeley, *The Wilderness of Dreams,* 185–186.

12. Daniel Prechtel, "To Have the Mind of Christ: Symbol Guidance and the Development of Communal Spiritual Discernment Processes for Parish Life, Mission, and Ministry," D.Min. thesis, Seabury-Western Theological Seminary, 2002, p. 32.

13. Jeremy Taylor, *Where People Fly and Water Runs Uphill: Using Dreams to Tap the Wisdom of the Unconscious* (New York: Time Warner, 1992), 72, 134–135.

14. Taylor, *Where People Fly and Water Runs Uphill,* 166–167.

15. Some of their story is described in the book *The Community Dream: Awakening the Christian Tribal Consciousness* by Pat C. Brockman, O.S.U., Ph.D. (Boulder: WovenWord Press, 2000). Brockman, who consulted with this S.S.J. community, also documents other communities' engagement in communal dreamwork.

Chapter 5:
Groups for Building a
Spiritual Community of Support

1. This collect from St. Gregory's Abbey, Three Rivers, Michigan, is typical of prayers commemorating Benedict.

2. Chittister, *Rule of Benedict,* Prologue.

3. The Psalter, *The Book of Common Prayer* (1979), 649.

4. Joan Scanlon, O.P., later became a leader of her order, the Kentucky Dominicans, and executive director and president of the Dominican Alliance.

5. Because this was a course where students took turns leading the group and I served as participant-mentor to the group, we often had an extensive

process review following the close of the group session rather than just before closing the group, which I advocate when it is not a training session.

6. Based on a 1996 Chicago Men's Conference workshop presentation by Bill Kauth, who also refers to James Hillman, Richard Rohr, and Thomas Moore.

Chapter 6:
Groups for Compassion
and Social Action

1. *Psalter for the Christian People,* ed. Gordon Lathrop and Gail Ramshaw (Collegeville: The Liturgical Press, 1993).

2. "An Outline of the Faith, commonly called the Catechism," *The Book of Common Prayer* (1979), 861. See also "Ministration to the Sick," 453–461.

3. See their website at http://dev.orderofstluke.org/.

4. *The Book of Common Prayer* (1979), 133.

5. *The Book of Common Prayer* (1979), 456.

6. *The Book of Common Prayer* (1979), 302.

7. "Celebration for a Home," *The Book of Occasional Services 2003* (New York: Church Hymnal Corporation, 2004), 147.

8. The following is the statement concerning exorcism: "The practice of expelling evil spirits by means of prayer and set formulas derives its authority from the Lord himself who identified these acts as signs of his messiahship. Very early in the life of the Church the development and exercise of such rites were reserved to the bishop, at whose discretion they might be delegated to selected presbyters and others deemed competent. In accordance with this established tradition, those who find themselves in need of such a ministry should make the fact known to the bishop, through their parish priest, in order that the bishop may determine whether exorcism is needed, who is to perform the rite, and what prayers or other formularies are to be used." "Concerning Exorcism," *The Book of Occasional Services,* 174.

9. Sacramental theology would see the primary sacraments of Holy Baptism and Holy Eucharist as efficacious for movements toward deep healing and wholeness of individuals, *communities,* and the world. This healing movement includes deliverance on many levels.

10. *The Book of Common Prayer* (1979), 305.

11. At the time of writing, the United States is trying to recover from the Great Recession and to extricate itself from wars on two fronts: Iraq and Afghanistan. There have been minimal guidelines agreed upon at an international gathering in Copenhagen on setting goals for global warming. Many nations, including the United States, still face considerable opposition to significant carbon emissions reduction policies and treaty ratifications.

12. Robert McAfee Brown, *Spirituality and Liberation: Overcoming the Great Fallacy* (Louisville: Westminster Press, 1988).

13. The Latin American Christian base community movement began in the 1960s as a way for a small group to gather for reflection on the Bible with an application to particular situations with a view toward a theology of liberation.

14. Grenz, ed., *In Dialogue with Scripture,* 90–91.

Chapter 7:
Leading a Small Group

1. An insight from family systems theory is that all people in the system interact with each other and affect the system. When two people in the system are in a disagreement, there is a tendency for one of the people to try and bring a third person onto their side. For example, someone (A) in a group might be unhappy about another group member (B) and may go to the leader or someone else (C) to complain and try to get an ally to put additional pressure on the second person to change. The desired ally (C) is being triangled into the situation. However, the person who is being triangled (C) can become a helpful agent for the situation if he or she refuses to take sides but instead offers to serve as a mediator assisting the two people (A and B) in discussing the situation and seeking a mutual resolution.

2. From a handout at The Upper Room Academy #5.

3. See Eric H. F. Law, *The Wolf Shall Dwell with the Lamb: A Spirituality for Leadership in a Multicultural Community* (St. Louis: Chalice Press, 1993), chap. 9.

4. Spiritual Directors International provides a copy of its ethical guidelines to new members. Additional copies can be ordered through the website at http://sdiworld.org. In a Web search the following links were readily accessed as examples of ethical guidelines: the Australian Ecumenical Council for Spiritual Direction Code of Ethics for Spiritual Directors at http://spiritualdirection.org.au/index2.php?option=com_content&do_pdf=1&id=26; and the Evangelical Spiritual Directors Association Code of Ethics at http://www.ecswisdom.org/index.php/esda/code-of-ethics.

5. Spiritual Directors International's website has an "Enrichment, Formation, and Training Program Locator" at http://sdiworld.org/programs-locator.html.

Chapter 8:
Special Applications

1. See John Lionberger's Renewal in the Wilderness website at http://www.renewalinthewilderness.org.

2. The Shem Center's website is http://web.me.com/shemcenter1/_shem_web/Shem_Welcome.html.

3. See http://www.dancesofuniversalpeace.org/home.shtm.

4. The Zeller and McGovern statements from "Statements of Group Spiritual Companionship 2009 Class Members on their Projects and Next Steps,"

posted on the Institute of Spiritual Companionship website at
http://iofsc.org/index.php?pr=GSCProgram.

5. E-mail from Cliff Haggenjos to the author, dated March 25, 2008. Used by
permission.

6. Diane Millis was a workshop presenter at the Spiritual Directors
International Conference in Atlanta in May 2011. In the workshop she led,
she asked me to be the storyteller and requested that I briefly address two
questions: If my life were a book, what title would I give it? What chapter
title would I give for what is going on presently in my life? She subsequently
gave me permission to use the material I have included here. The Journey
Conversations Project website is http://www.journeyconversations.org/.

Conclusion:
Gathered in the
Name of the Divine

1. Paul uses the language of the community having the mind of Christ in two
passages: 1 Corinthians 2:12–16 and Philippians 2:1–11.

2. John Mabry, e-mail correspondence to the author, dated November 5,
2010. Used by permission.

3. One version of this story shows up as the Prologue to M. Scott Peck's *The
Different Drum* (New York: Touchstone, 1998). Online searches of key
words "one of you is the messiah" or "the rabbi's gift" will show other
versions. I first encountered this as oral tradition—I think it was told to me at
a conference in the 1970s by Megan McKenna.

4. St. Irenaeus, second-century bishop of Lyons, is often quoted as saying,
"The glory of God is a person fully human, fully alive." The full quotation is
a little more complex and speaks of the glory as God's connection to the
human: "The glory of God is man fully alive, and the life of man is the vision
of God. If the revelation of God through creation already brings life to all
living beings on the earth, how much more will the manifestation of the
Father by the Word bring life to those who see God" (*Adversus Haereses* IV,
20, 7). However, the idea that becoming fully ourselves is God's intention
and glory is also hinted at in Hasidic oral tradition. In various forms Rabbi
Zusia is said to have exclaimed after a vision of angels or a Heavenly
Tribunal, "When the time comes for me to die and stand before the Lord, the
Lord will not question me about why I was not more like Moses or Abraham.
Instead, the Lord will ask me why I was not more fully Zusia." The version
above was said to me in a presentation at the Institute of Spiritual
Companionship. On the Reb Zusia (Rav Zussye) saying see, for example,
http://www.flickr.com/photos/mazalart/2488525819/ or
http://www.theagelesswisdom.com/AbolishWar/quotes1.html.

Appendix:
Spiritual Exercises for
Circle of the Spirit Groups and Retreats

1. Adapted from Gerald G. May, *Pilgrimage Home: The Conduct of Contemplative Practice in Groups* (Mahwah, N.J.: Paulist Press, 1979), 120.

2. I first heard this beautiful meditation as part of a class presentation at the Institute of Spiritual Companionship. I apologize for my inability to remember who led that meditation.

3. I learned this from Gerald May at a Spiritual Directors International conference when he led the conferees in this prayer exercise.

4. May, *Pilgrimage Home,* 125–126.

5. The Psalter, *The Book of Common Prayer* (1979), 794–795.

6. Adapted from a meditation given by Flora Wuellner at The Upper Room Academy of Spiritual Formation #5 in Madison, Wisconsin.

7. Nikos Kazantzakis, *Report to Greco* (New York: Bantam Books, 1966), 143.

8. Adapted for a group focus from "Finding a Buried Treasure," in Carolyn Stahl Bohler, *Opening to God: Guided Imagery Meditation on Scripture,* revised and expanded edition (Nashville: The Upper Room, 1996), 58–59.

9. I am indebted to Brother Joseph Kilikevice of the Shem Center for Interfaith Spirituality for introducing me to this practice.

10. I first ran across Scripture role play reading Walter Wink, *Transforming Bible Study* (Nashville: Abingdon Press, 1988), 118–119. See also his chapter 8, "Engaging the Other Side of the Brain," which provides many modes of engaging Scripture in transformative ways.

11. A directee taught me this exercise many years ago, saying that he used it at the end of each day as a spiritual *examen.*

CPSIA information can be obtained
at www.ICGtesting.com
Printed in the USA
BVHW032159270921
617665BV00006B/68